Collins

need to know?

DJ Tips

Collins

First published in 2007 by Collins
an imprint of
HarperCollins Publishers
77–85 Fulham Palace Road
London W6 8JB

www.collins.co.uk

Collins is a registered trademark of
HarperCollins Publishers Limited

10 09 08 07
6 5 4 3 2 1

A catalogue record for this book is available from
the British Library

Created by **Focus Publishing**, Sevenoaks, Kent
Project editor: Guy Croton
Designer and illustrator: Diarmuid Moloney
Series design: Mark Thomson
Front cover photograph: Matthew Smith, PYMCA
Back cover photographs: Point Blank; Ministry of Sound

ISBN-13: 978 000 724632 8
ISBN-10: 000 724632 3

Printed and bound by Printing Express Ltd, Hong Kong

Disclaimer
This book is not a substitute for independent legal
advice and no liability can be accepted by the author
or the publishers for anything done in reliance on
matters referred to in this book. The doing of an
unauthorized act in relation to a copyright work
may result in a civil claim for damages and/or
criminal prosecution.

For Mishy, Molly, Casey and Ruby.
A massive thanks to Rob Cowan and an extra Big Up
to Anoushka India.

Contents

Introduction

Legend has it that Punk Rock was so pervasive in the late 1970s that, if you got into a taxicab in London or New York, the driver played guitar. Now, thirty years later, the driver's a DJ. Universal DJ Culture has taken hold.

DJ Culture

The phenomenon of modern DJ Culture, which, like so many forms of popular music, started in the 1980s in the north of England, has seen a nonstop rise in popularity ever since. Back then, working class kids tried to imitate the music they were hearing from America, and more specifically, Chicago. 'Dance Music' has become the international language of youth and is perhaps the only thing that unites young people in every country on earth. Any club night in San Francisco, London, Moscow or Beijing looks and sounds pretty much the same and, without exception, always centres on the undisputed star of the show: the DJ. Every pop star wants in on the action and, as people who were young in the 1980s

Superstar DJ... DJ Blame (left) and DJ Booker T (right) are each big names in the world of DJing, and both hugely influential.

grow into the establishment, bankers, lawyers and even politicians are coming out as former DJs with fond memories of dancing and playing out in clubs, pubs, bars and Acid House raves.

Carl Cox (left) is a DJ legend and king of cool scratching techniques. Basement Jaxx (above, seated) is another major league name.

So you want to be a DJ?

This book contains everything you need to know to join the party. If you don't already own any DJ equipment, then you should read the first chapter before you start spending. If you do have some gear, then you will soon learn how to get the most out of what you've got. Of course you don't own enough records yet (that would be impossible) so in any case you have some shopping to do.

DJing, like music itself, can inspire and fill the souls of the DJ and everyone enjoying their performance. And DJing, like music itself, has no rules (or should have none, anyway) but this book provides all the guidance, tips, information and inspiration you need to know to set you on your way. Happy spinning.

1 The essential gear

Without quality gear, no DJ can put on a quality show. The 'quality' of DJing gear, however, does not refer necessarily to any particular brand name or top of the range item – some of the best mixes are done on old, out-of-date or seriously cheap sound systems. The best gear for any DJ is whatever gear they have come to know and love and respect. Any combination of equipment can be the right tools, provided those tools are that DJ's Essential Gear.

Vinyl records

As one of mankind's greatest inventions, the vinyl record is still the world's best music storage system, offering the best and most satisfying sound quality for reproduction of recorded music.

Cool vinyl

Put simply, with the right gear properly set up and skilfully used, nothing sounds as good as a vinyl record. Another crucially important feature of vinyl records is that the DJ can literally 'see', and therefore spontaneously interact with, the music – that is, the grooves – on the record. This physical aspect of vinyl is probably the main factor in the historical development of DJing.

Vinyl records are an 'analogue' storage medium, which means that an 'analogy' of the sound is physically stamped into the vinyl. The physical soundwaves which form the sound coming out of, say, a person's mouth when they sing, are first converted by a microphone into an electronic signal and later converted by a record cutting machine (called a 'lathe') into large, small, wide and narrow grooves on the record. When played on a turntable, the needle (stylus) 'rides' the grooves and, put simply, translates the left-right and up-down movements into loud/soft, high/low and left/right stereo signals. The speakers then convert these signals back into physical soundwaves. The first people ever to hear vinyl records played thought they were witnessing a miracle, which is roughly the same sensation that a DJ can create on a good night.

Your box of tunes is the key to the success of your set. You can never have too many vinyl records – so keep on buying them.

Handle your vinyl records carefully - even when you are flat-out in the middle of a set - because without gentle care they will deteriorate very quickly.

The disadvantages of vinyl records

The great disadvantage of vinyl records is that, like humans, they deteriorate over time. If great care is taken, the deterioration can be minimized and slowed but, in the end, nothing can stop them eventually wearing out. The worst news of all is that the best way to preserve a vinyl record is to not play it at all - a cruel irony obviously created by the Devil (or, perhaps, the God of Digital Music). Best practice to maximize the life of a vinyl record includes:

- Minimal handling, and then only on its edge or the centre label.
- Upright storage (on its edge) with inner sleeves of paper or plastic.
- Storage in a moderate and reasonably constant temperature.
- Use only on a properly setup turntable with a properly weighted stylus.
- Occasional dust cleaning, if necessary, with a dedicated cleaning kit or with isopropyl ('rubbing') alcohol, using very light pressure.

Turntables

A turntable, also known as a 'deck', a 'record deck', a 'record player' or the 'wheels of steel', is the main tool of the DJ. Without a turntable, a DJ is nothing.

The development of the turntable

Having changed very little since its invention in Germany in 1888, the turntable is basically just a spinning platter and a tone arm with a needle-sharp stylus that drags through the grooves in the vinyl record. The 'platter' is the flat metal dish (made from aluminium on an expensive deck or from sheet metal on a cheap deck, which tends to warp), with a rubber top on which the record lays. The 'tone arm' is the stick along the right side that moves on a pivot with a counterweight on the back end. The 'stylus' (or 'needle') is the tiny piece of metal on the end of the tone arm, usually diamond-tipped, which sits inside a plastic housing called a 'cartridge'. Older turntables sometimes use special styli which can be difficult to install, but most modern decks can use any cartridge-based stylus, which are all so easy to install that many DJs can do emergency replacements of a stylus in the middle of their set without missing a beat.

Turntable controls

A turntable has a only a very small number of controls, each of which is mostly self-explanatory: the on/off button, the start/stop switch, the speed switch (for 33 or 45 rpm) and the pitch control for fine speed adjustments. Some decks have a 'speed check' feature: tiny bumps on the side of the platter which are illuminated by a small

must know

Even if you prefer CD Players or PC DJing, it's worth honing your skills on turntables, as in most clubs you will still find a pair of Technics which may be the only option or could save you in an emergency. And, in any case, all DJing is based on vinyl fundamentals, so this knowledge can only help, regardless of what you end up using in your set-up.

The Technics SL1200 is the DJ's turntable of choice – a standard part of DJing kit since the 1980s.

light and, when the dots appear stationary, show that the platter is spinning at the correct rate.

Types of turntable

The two main types of turntable are the 'belt drive' and the 'direct drive'; each term describes how the motor turns the platter. It is often said that the lack of a rubber belt or chain in a direct drive deck (where the motor directly drives the platter without any intermediary), creates a more consistent and more reliable revolution of the disc. However, in practice this isn't always true and you shouldn't put too much stock into this distinction.

Without a shadow of a doubt, the most commonly used turntable is the Technics 1210 Mark II (or, possibly, the older Mark 1 version usually known simply as the '1210', or the 2002 version called the 'Mark III' which adds only an improved pitch control). These decks have been the industry standard since the 1980s and are favoured by most DJs. A close runner-up, however, is the Vestax PDX-d3 (and the similar models PDX-a1, PDT-a2 'Scratch', and the PDT-5000). The main advantages of the PDX-d3 are its digital control mechanism and a surprisingly handy reverse play mode. Another serious competitor is Numark, a well-known DJ gear company that also produces a fine range of modern decks.

CD players

There are still some DJs that deny the existence of CD players in clubs, but the majority embraced them years ago and many use nothing else. Like everything, they have their pros and cons.

The advantages of CD players

The main advantage of the CD player is the CD which, even if it does not sound quite as 'warm' as its vinyl equivalent and cannot be directly manipulated with a finger, lasts a lot longer and weighs an awful lot less. These points are pretty important to DJs who hate having to replace their vinyl records over and over, and could never actually hand-carry 250 vinyl records to a gig in Amsterdam (because, of course, you could never check-in your tunes as airline baggage, any more than you could check-in your baby sister). While CDs do tend to last for years, they are still vulnerable to the same dirty problems if not cared for – and the results can easily be worse: a careless fingerprint can cause a very loud and nasty glitch or a seriously un-funky clicking skip. It is therefore important to regularly clean and carefully handle your CDs, though simple storage in a CD wallet is far more convenient than cumbersome vinyl and will not harm the discs.

CD player features

The basic CD player has only the most simple features: stop, start, rewind, fast-forward and pause – with possibly a pitch control on the slightly more up-market decks. The best DJ CD players now have loads of features, including auto-looping, edit and cue functions and memory facilities to store cues

The key component of a DJ CD player is the 'wheel' at the centre of the machine which enables the DJ to control the movement of the CD like a vinyl record.

and play multiple tracks, even from different discs, in succession. The key development, however, is the big plastic 'wheel' on top of the deck which allows the DJ to control the CD with their finger with an amazingly vinyl-like feel (and even to scratch).

The drawbacks of CD players

Since the launch of specialized CD DJ models in the late 1990s (also casually known as 'decks' or 'CD decks'), CD players are installed in almost all clubs and have become a fundamental tool for the modern DJ. Of course, the main drawback to mixing on CD players is that, unlike the grooves on vinyl, the DJ cannot physically see the music and must instead rely on electronic features to find a chosen song (or bit of a song) and to adjust the speed of the music.

MP3 and other digital audio files

DJs who think a CD is just a weak version of a vinyl record are likely to regard a digital audio file as a complete non-starter: both the storage disc and the music are entirely invisible and the sound quality, at least in the case of MP3s, is far worse than that of a CD.

Why use them?

For a more open-minded DJ, however, digital audio files present so many new advantages that they make both vinyl and CD seem like Grandpa's ancient and boring baby toys.

A digital audio file is a single chunk of computer data comprising one piece of music – usually one song. As with computers in general, there is a large and ever-increasing number of different formats available for digital audio files – and an equally large number of software programs available to play them on. The professional pop music world relies on the best possible quality formats (such as .aiff and .wav, which unfortunately use massive amounts of data and quickly fill a computer's memory) and the most flexible sophisticated programs (such as ProTools, Logic and Cubase). Most music fans, however, prefer the easy stuff: MP3s and MP3 players.

Apple Macintosh's iPod has completely changed the way that many DJs now operate. An entire set can be cued up and played on this tiny and ingenious device.

Advantages of MP3 files

To be sure, an 'MP3' (which is short for 'Moving Pictures Expert Group, Layer 3') is a digital audio file, but one in which the music has been 'compressed' and therefore uses a very small amount of data. Often this is as little as three megabytes, or about one-tenth of its original un-compressed version. While this means the sound quality

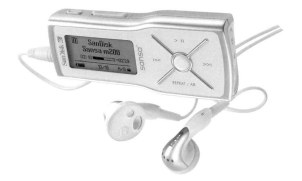

Even if you choose not to use an MP3 player when performing your mix, it's a great way to check out new tunes and decide what you are going to play.

has been reduced, it also means that far more files – that is, songs – can be stored on a small computer (a laptop, or an MP3 Player such as an iPod). Additionally, those files can be moved around, manipulated very quickly and easily and shared instantly via the internet. For many DJs, this is not a compromise, but a much needed and exciting revolution.

The possibilities for mixing MP3s (or any other format of digital audio files) are endless: finding spots in the music is a doddle; anything you find or do can be saved forever for later instant recall; speed and pitch can be changed in any way (and can be adjusted independently); and the variations are limitless.

As for the 'quality' question, most DJs either ignore the issue – and dancing audiences generally do not complain about MP3 quality – or they go the extra mile by using some other, better-quality, format than MP3s. These include .aiff, .wav and the proprietary formats like .aac of Apple or the various Sony formats.

It seems almost quaint to mention it but, as every member of the iPod generation knows very well, thousands and thousands of tunes can be easily carried in one hand – stored in the memory of your laptop, MP3 player, or on a single CD-style data storage disc.

PC DJ and digital gear

The marriage of computers and DJing probably started in the 1990s with the launch of the original software program named 'WinAmp', that could playback digital audio files in any order. It was also very easy to use, which added to its popularity.

Rip, burn and listen

Within a few years, most computers came with a 'soundcard' ready-installed. This allowed for quite good-quality direct digital transfers of music from their old CDs into digital music files stored on the computer's internal memory (known as 'ripping'), then from the internal memory onto blank CDs (known as 'burning'), and finally from the computer itself to the speakers, in a way that sounded, at least to the average music fan's ears, just like their sitting room hi-fi system (known as 'listening'). Some of the new 'computer music' fans were already proper DJs and began demanding new and better ways to rip, burn and listen to their fast-growing libraries of digital audio files (which were mostly MP3s).

With a good CD burner, you can organize your tunes any way you see fit and then get them onto a disc of your own making.

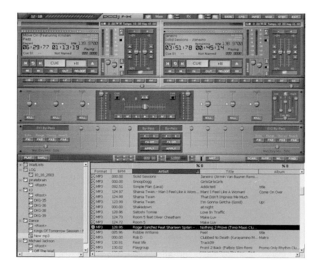

A screen shot of the original PCDJ digital music editing program, which has been available to DJs since the 1990s.

Unsurprisingly, many companies launched new products to meet this demand.

One of the earliest, and perhaps the first serious computer-based DJ tool, was the 'PCDJ' program, released by Digital 1 Media in the 1990s. PCDJ, with its various updates, continues to be a powerful way to control, mix and match – in real-time – digital audio files (as well as digital video files) and is widely used by DJs all over the world. The software has all the very useful features now commonly available on computer music mixing programs, including: easy-to-use rip and burn facilities; automatic speed and pitch matching and adjustment; the automatic insertion of up to 20 basic cue point positions into each individual song.

Another key advantage of computer mixing is the combination and ease of use of other digital gear, such as digital mixers. There are also accessories for special effects which can cheaply and easily add loads of new features to a mix, including standard effects such as delay and sampling in digital form, and newfangled effects that can barely be described – all within the touch of a few buttons.

Mixers

Mixers (or, as music shops tend to call them, 'disco mixers') are perhaps the second most important tool of the DJ. Whatever format you choose to mix (vinyl records, CDs, MP3s), you must have a mixer.

Vestax mixers like the one pictured below will do everything that the average DJ desires in order to fine-tune their sound.

Mixer functions

Mixers exist as the conventional physical kind, with knobs and faders, and as the digital kind, as part of your computer music program. At its most basic, a bog-standard mixer has two functions: it boosts the relatively weak electronic signal that comes out of the turntables/CD players/MP3 Players to a level high enough for power amplifiers, and it allows the DJ to choose, mix and balance the turntables/CD players/MP3 Players and, at the same time, monitor them through headphones. Mixers are sometimes referred to as 'pre-amplifiers' because they serve the function of strengthening the signal before it goes to the amplifier – and this is an important point because, if you use turntables, a 'pre-amp' must always be used to 'bump up', that is amplify, the signal. In short, remember that you must always plug a turntable into the 'phono' input on a mixer because that input has the strongest pre-amp (see more on this in Chapter 2, page 38).

Choosing a mixer

Choosing a mixer is a very personal decision and the most important criteria is often something very individual, such as the size or the feel of the faders or the overall look of the mixer (after all, a DJ is a performer to their public). There are many combinations of features available on the various makes and models of mixers but, at the very least, you must have:

- At least two channels (but three or more is better) and ideally with a 'gain' and 'EQ' on each.
- A 'crossfader' (which is easily removable for DIY servicing).
- A 'phono/line' switch for each channel (if buying second-hand, check these to make sure they don't crackle).
- VU meters (either needles or lights), ideally assignable to AFL or PFL.
- A master volume fader (if buying second-hand, check to make sure it doesn't crackle).
- A robust headphone socket with its own adjustable volume for monitoring.

While a basic mixer with only the above features would suffice, recommended models include the Pioneer DJ500M and the Vestax PMC-50A, PMC-40 and PMC-17A. For the ambitious DJ with plans to perform 'scratching', the Vestax PMC-05PRO or PMC-07PRO are top of the range models, while DJs intending to compete (or 'battle') should consider the Technics SH DJ 1200.

One of the most important aspects of a DJ's set-up is that it must have a separate system for listening to (or 'monitoring') any source of music on headphones for the DJ to listen privately without the audience hearing, so that the right point to start (or 'cue up') the next tune can be found. This is usually done through the headphone jack on the mixer itself or through a special monitor speaker. Very occasionally, you will find a special monitor system with a monitor amp and a monitor speaker in the DJ booth for this purpose.

must know

The Vestax PMC-07PRO is widely regarded as the best scratch mixer ever made, and boasts 'quadraphonic' capability as each channel has four outputs.

Speakers, amplifiers and crossovers

A mixer combines and balances your tunes but, unless headphone listening is all you ever want, you will still need some way to hear your mix. Just about everyone knows that speakers put out the sound, but fewer people know much about amplifiers, which power the speakers.

Different set-ups

The most basic set-up will use only one amp and two speakers which each have a single actual speaker cone (the cone-shaped paper hat-type-things that make the air move) inside them. A more sophisticated (and better-sounding) system will use speakers with at least two actual speaker cones in each cabinet, known as a 'woofer' and a 'tweeter'. This will therefore require at least two amplifiers – one to power the woofer and one to power the tweeter – and a 'crossover' to separate the music. This means that the woofer and its amp get only the low sounds and the tweeter and its amp get only the high sounds.

In most cases, the punter never sees these components because they are hidden inside the self-contained units, but it helps to remember and know why your sound quality will improve with the more sophisticated set-up.

When practising at home, just about any HiFi system will do, although a dedicated power amp and proper large-ish speakers (or self-amplified speakers) tend to sound a lot better.

The simple approach

For a cheap and cheerful result, just use your existing home HiFi system by plugging the main stereo outputs on the back of your mixer (probably labeled 'Main Out' or 'Record Out') into the 'line' input of your home system. However, keep in mind: this method often bypasses the 'master fader' on your mixer and sends a very loud level into your home system, so keep the HiFi volume all the way down until you get an idea of how loud it all is.

A separate woofer and tweeter will usually make for a better speaker.

Other essential DJ equipment

There are a few other essential items of kit that every DJ needs – from the DJ's trademark headphones ('cans') to spare needles and other bits and pieces that enable them to ply their trade.

Cans

Headphones, or 'cans', are the most vulnerable of the DJ's tools because they tend to get dropped, kicked, thrown about and lost very often. You can use any headphones in the world for DJing (and you probably will) but always remember that they will rarely last long – so try not to spend too much on them. Just be sure that they are plenty loud enough and that they fully enclose your ears (though they are often used on only one ear) to shut out all background noise.

Needles (styli)

Virtually every turntable will come with a cartridge in it, but remember that every stylus is likely to be either too cheap, too worn or both – or will be very soon. You will therefore need a back-up to carry with you at all times, for those annoying DJ emergencies.

Slipmats

A 'slipmat' is the piece of material that fits over your platter to stop the rubber top of your platter from 'gripping' the record. While this is completely pointless and quite counter-intuitive to a normal vinyl user, it is crucial to a DJ because the art depends on being able to move the record independently of the motor and against the direction the platter is spinning. Slipmats are cheap and are available in all sizes, shapes, and

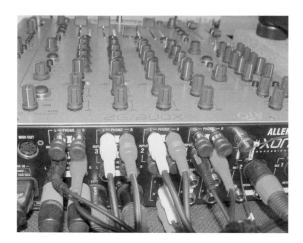

Your equipment needs to be reliably hooked-up at all times, so invest in the best leads you can afford.

designs (though most are round and black). The only thing that really matters for a slipmat is that it slips a lot.

Wires

As you will see in later chapters, there can be a lot of wires involved in DJing and you are very likely to buy loads of leads and connectors during your DJ career. The best advice is: don't skimp. Hefty and long leads with solid metal connectors are almost always worth the extra expense.

FX boxes

'FX' units (or 'special effects boxes') can be a useful and very enjoyable DJ tool for both the DJ and their audience. Versions of FX boxes include: reverb, delay, chorus, flangers, compressors, gates, samplers, looping effects and EQ. With increasing frequency, FX boxes tend to feature more than one of these effects – and sometimes all of them. A key rule to remember is: the fewer effects a single FX box features, the more unique and flexible it is likely to be.

want to know more?

- Visit your local music shop (useful for browsing and trying out different models)
- See: http://www.stanton dj.com/v2/index.asp for Stanton gear
- Visit: http://www.panasonic .co.uk/technics-dj-home/index.htm for Technics turntables
- The official 1210 website is at www.technics1210. com
- Tips for buying gear can be found at http://www.dj-tips-and-tricks.com/

2 Getting started

So now you know what stuff is available, the burning issues become: 'where can I get all the essential gear that I need – and how do I set it all up?' As with everything else, it's very easy once you know how and, luckily, this chapter has all the answers in one place. Of course, before putting your sound system together you must decide generally what sort of DJ you want to be. It's no good buying a classic turntable and then discovering that you prefer CDs, and it is even worse to start by spending loads of money on classic MP3s before deciding that you are a turntablist at heart. If you really cannot decide, don't fret: most of the information in this chapter applies to all styles and systems. Just make sure you don't blow your budget too soon.

Buying music

Every DJ obviously has a great love of music – and probably for many different styles. However, to be a truly brilliant turntablist, you need to pin your colours to the mast of some particular genre. This will enable you to develop an expertise and carve out a home within the DJ army and the huge range of music that people can dance to.

Know your style

The best Dream Gear in the world is useless without tunes. Trouble is, you have to know what genre you are – and what kind of gear you use – before you can start buying.

Every good DJ must listen to as much music from as many different styles as possible at all times. Obviously, as you are a serious music lover, this is no hardship. But, as a DJ, it is your duty and solemn vow to forever continue your musical education and keep abreast of new music. You owe it to yourself and to your audience, just as a concert pianist owes it to their audience to keep practising.

Check out the CD and vinyl racks at all the best local music shops on a regular basis. It is vital to keep abreast of what is going on right across the music spectrum.

For the widest range of music, it is best to take a trip to a DJ or vinyl specialist shop - or just the biggest record shop you can find.

The best place to hear new music and experience new performances is in the DJ's concert hall: clubs, bars and wherever good DJs play out. If you aren't able, for whatever reason, to get to those places often enough or at all, the next best options are record shops and websites that feature wide-ranging catalogues and plenty of new music. Spending time in DJ-orientated record shops is especially useful if you are able to meet other DJs and talk about music and performance, and witness people actually spinning.

The most popular DJ, even if they are skilled and tricky, will always be known primarily for the style of music they play. Accordingly, you will have to choose a style and/or genre to make your own. There are hundreds of genres and sub-genres and sub-sub-genres of music in the world to choose from, but most choose more than one in combination, in pursuit of a fresh and unique sound.

The most important thing is that, whatever you choose, you really have to love it. Never choose music just because it's popular. If you don't love what you play out, you'll probably never achieve greatness - and you may even end up hating DJing.

DANCE MUSIC GENRES

ACID – Acid House is the mother of modern dance music because it was the first to combine funky danceable beats with serious technology. The defining elements of Acid House are: the caustic, metallic, 'acidic' noises that come from the original Roland TR303; big breakdowns; and simple beats (usually four-on-the-floor).

AMBIENT – Used loosely, this word usually means the music is sparse or that it features long, meandering sections with few beats and hardly any music. Usually using samples from movie soundtracks and avant-garde pop records, DJs like Sasha and John Digweed helped turn this genre into a worldwide movement in the Nineties. The wide spaces in the music make it easy to mix.

BIG BEAT – Usually with a House or Garage-style tempo and using beats and samples which would not be out of place in a Hip Hop record, Fatboy Slim almost single-handedly brought this genre to the mainstream.

DEEP HOUSE – As another style of early Dance Music, Deep House originated in Chicago and is closely related to House and Acid, though it tends to use more vocals and instruments in particularly soulful and funky features.

DISCO – Think of Disco as less a genre than an attitude, an element and an inspiration. Loads of modern music, from Manchester to Madonna, incorporates Disco beats, samples and songs. However, because so many original Disco records from the 1970s tend to sound quite thin and tinny against the huge bass sounds of today, many old Disco records have been re-worked to beef up the sounds, with great success.

DRUM'n'BASS – As a product of Jungle, D'n'B is fast and furious. The beats are frenetic, the song structures are free and unpredictable, and DJs playing D'n'B have to stay alert to avoid musical car crashes.

HARD HOUSE – Combining the wild and nasty big rave synth sounds of the early Nineties with banging Techno beats, Hard House generally appeals to younger audiences that have the energy to keep up and the ability to put up with Hoover noises.

HOUSE – House, the first modern style of dance music to achieve mainstream recognition, is the most basic and effective music for a novice DJ to mix because the beats are straightforward and the songs are structured in uniformly-square and easily-predictable chunks of round numbers of bars. UK House was the music of legendary 'Madchester' and the famous club, the Hacienda. US House and Garage was brought to the wider public by DJs in New York such as Todd Terry in the late Eighties. The best thing about this music for novice DJs is that if you lose your place in a House record, you can just wait for it to come round again – which it always does in another 8 or 16 bars.

R'n'B – R'n'B is, in fact, Soul music with Hip-Hop beats, funky rhythms and/or Rap. This genre can be harder to mix because it requires keen awareness and judgement of vocals, melody and musical structure. But then, of course, you get to listen to loads of seriously soulful tunes and killer vocals.

RAGGA – Reggae fans can easily get hooked on this style if they dig the rapped vocals called 'toasting'. The tempos tend to vary widely, which can make it difficult to mix unless you carefully choose your set and work hard.

RAP – The trouble with Rap records for DJs is that there are virtually no rules: anything goes. The tunes tend to stop randomly, change tempo in the middle and generally ambush the DJ. Again, you have to carefully choose your set and work hard.

TECHNO – The combination of electro-pop and House yielded this quite minimal of four-to-the-floor genres. Classic Techno features wild modern sci-fi sounds and aggressive machine noises. Done well, this can be a joy to mix. Done badly, it may give everyone in the audience a migraine.

TRANCE & PROGRESSIVE – Born out of Nineties European psychedelia and closely related to Ambient, Trance mostly features relentless pulsing synth sequences designed to induce hypnosis. It's easy and fun and well-suited to beginners.

UK GARAGE – Soulful vocals on top of rough Drum'n'Bass-style basslines with swinging beats adds up to a top choice for a novice DJ, especially as it lends itself to easy mixing using the basic techniques and tricks.

Buying equipment

The golden rule 'try everything in life once' certainly applies when buying a sound system. Don't be put off by what other people tell you: experiment, take your time and arrive at your own decision as to what works for you.

Test-driving gear

Your first move should be to knock up each of your DJ friends and finagle your way onto their gear for a nice long test run. If you don't feel you know enough even to try it on, ask your mate to take you through the paces so you can check it out at close range. Once you have exhausted your supply of geared-up pals, get on down to the music shops and work your way through the range from the bottom up. Of course it helps to actually buy something when trying to get enthusiastic help from music shop staff but, even if you buy nothing, there is no harm in trying.

Buying second-hand

The best trick, however, is not to buy anything from *any* shop at *any* time. Provided you are not in too much of a hurry and are willing to read a thousand small ads in a dozen papers, as well as trawl another thousand pages on a hundred websites, a brilliant system can be purchased very cheaply. When buying second-hand there is always the danger that things are not all that they seem but, so long as you don't pay too much for any one item, the risks are low. As a rule, you should never buy anything that you can't turn on and try out beforehand. Naturally you should check that all the faders slide and the knobs and wheels turn smoothly

try this

It is always useful to read the manuals of your equipment – it may be slow going and seem like a waste of time but you only have to read it once and then you'll have it somewhere in your DJ brain forever. Besides, every machine will have some quirk or special feature worth knowing.

Buy the best kit you can afford, but take your time and don't get stressed out if your mate's gear is better than yours.

and don't crackle, and that the backs and bottoms don't look too worn. Don't be too put off by dirty metal, however, as a quick wipe with a damp rag can do wonders – and use 'rubbing alcohol' (aka 'isopropyl') rather than water, because in small quantities it evaporates instantly and won't harm electronic gear.

Buying new

If money is no object (and pigs could fly), buying new is certainly the best option. For starters, you can take it back if you don't like it, or if it doesn't work. You are also more likely to get a later model and, conveniently, all the proper manuals to read when you have trouble sleeping.

Wherever you end up shopping, be sure to take your time, look for special sales and always ask in every shop if they have a sale coming on soon – or have just finished one. Plan carefully, and don't let anyone talk you out of following your plan or into making a rash decision. With a bit of luck – or, erm, maybe with quite a lot of luck – this could be the Dream Gear that you treasure for the rest of your life.

Hooking up

Like cricket, it's all about 'ins and outs' and there are plenty of each. Think of your sound system as a plumbing exercise: the 'water' (i.e. sound) must travel from the 'supply tank' (deck) through the 'pipes' (wires), first to the 'main intake' (mixer), and finally through each of the separate 'runs' (channels on the mixer) to the 'pumps' and 'taps' (amps and speakers).

The ins and outs of DJing

If that is too convoluted, try to remember at least that if there is no physical connection leading all the way from the source to the end, with good solid joins at each juncture, then the sound will not get to the speakers.

The short and easy version of getting the sound from DJ to dancefloor is as follows:

- Each turntable has a stereo audio lead coming out of it which gets connected to the PHONO inputs of the channel on the back of the mixer marked PHONO IN (or, if not marked, then just one of the channels). The ground (or 'earth') wire coming out of the back of the turntable gets connected to the earth point (usually a screw on the back of each channel, though a small mixer may have just one).

- If you are using CD Players, MP3 Players or a computer instead of a turntable, plug the stereo audio lead from each one (the OUT or OUTPUT) to the LINE IN inputs of a channel on the back of the mixer marked LINE (or, if not marked, then just one of the channels). CD players, MP3 Players and

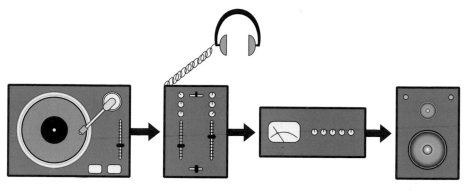

From left to right: turntable; mixer; amplifier; speaker. Turn each device on in this order to avoid damaging your system.

computers don't have 'earth' leads and need nothing else connected.

- The mixer now must be connected to the amp(s). Take a stereo lead and plug the main outputs of the mixer (left and right for stereo and probably marked 'MAIN OUT') into the main inputs of the power amp. If you're lucky enough to use a dedicated monitor amp for a monitor speaker in the DJ booth, then connect the mixer's 'Monitor Outputs' into that monitor amp, (but usually you'll just use the headphones coming straight from the mixer itself).

- Connect the amp(s) to the speakers.

- Finally, ensure that the turntable, the mixer and the amp(s) are all plugged into the wall for power.

Occasionally, you may find a club (or a posh mate) with a more complicated set-up which will probably involve a crossover, some sort of 'room EQ' and/or a set of two or three power amps that power the speakers in a 'two-way' or 'three-way' configuration. Don't worry about understanding it – just watch carefully, look confident and nod when they say it's a better set-up.

must know

The Vestax d3 turntable has a quartz lock function which fixes the deck speed at either 33 or 45 RPM, though it can be set at the much faster speed of 78 RPM by pressing both the 33 and 45 RPM buttons straight after turning on the deck.

Turning it on

Once you have plugged everything in and double-checked that the connections and the power leads are fitting snugly and are not being pulled on or strained, you can turn on each item in order of the flow of the 'water'.

Getting the flow right

- Turn on the turntables (and/or CD players, MP3 Players, or computer) first.
- Next, turn on the mixer.
- If you have them, turn on the crossover(s) and/or EQ(s) and monitor amps and monitor speaker(s).
- Finally, turn on the amp(s) for the main speakers.

By powering up in this order, and by leaving the amps until last, you ensure that no 'bump' is sent through the speakers (which could possibly be very loud and may damage the speakers). You should also get into the habit of checking that the volume knobs and faders are all down as far as they go when powering up. Never turn them up until everything is on and you are ready to react quickly by pulling or turning them down should any loud sounds, noises or feedback unexpectedly begin.

1 Once you have turned on your deck, CD or MP3 player, the next thing to activate is your mixer.

2 Make sure everything is hooked up properly at the back of the mixer if you have any problems getting it started.

3 When the mixer is activated, turn on your amplifier.

4 Again, if you have any problems, check the ports at the back of the amp to ensure the correct leads are in the right channels.

5 Finally, do the same thing with your speakers, making sure that the inputs are correctly hooked up.

Mechanical and electronic adjustments

Happily for DJs, there are usually no electronic adjustments that need to be made to any equipment before starting to mix. However, as in all walks of life, there are always exceptions to the usual rule. Here's what to watch out for.

The tone arm of your turntable needs to be correctly weighted in order to prevent the stylus from skipping on your records.

Beware electronic tweaks

Occasionally, if you are lucky enough to own (or find in a club) an overall EQ box and/or crossover for the sound system, someone will have to adjust the controls on each in a way that is best suited for the room the speakers are in. The same goes for the actual position of the speakers in the room, which can hugely affect the way the speakers sound. Unfortunately, these electronic adjustments are not at all easy to understand or, even for experts, to get right. So, unless you have done it many times before or have expert guidance, you will probably get a better sound by not touching the controls at all (that is, leaving them as they are, or at 'o').

Making mechanical tweaks

Mechanical adjustments are a completely different thing. Firstly, it is helpful to ensure that each piece of equipment (especially the turntable) is as level as possible, usually by using folded paper under one or two legs. Secondly, ensure that the weighting and height of your turntables' tone arms are correctly set for optimum performance. The aim is for you to be able to DJ without the stylus jumping out of the groove, but without using so much weight that your records suffer unnecessary wear and tear.

Start by calibrating the weight setting. To do this, let the tone arm hang by the side of the platter at just about the spot where the outer edge of a record would be (if it were there). Screw the weight well up the tone arm and then gradually take weight off by slowly screwing it back in the other direction, until the needle hangs at just about the height of the grooves (if a record were there). When the tone arm hangs balanced, set the free-spinning number-marked wheel to 'o' and use this as your null point. Now you can apply as much weight as recommended in the manufacturers' manual.

Now calibrate the height of the tone arm, which can be (slightly) raised to increase the force, or 'torque', on the needle. While this can help a very jumpy needle, torque-ing up is often a bad idea because most DJ cartridges need a flat tone arm for best all-round performance.

watch out!

Many turntables are strategically designed with rubber or foam feet to minimize vibrations, so don't create unnecessary problems for yourself by setting up on wobbly tables.

The weight of the tone arm can be accurately calibrated using the dials shown. Follow the manufacturer's instructions for the correct settings.

Faders and switches

When not in use, the faders, knobs, buttons and switches should be kept all the way down or off. After you have connected the gear and turned everything on, start by playing a tune and pushing the mixer's master fader(s) up to 'o' (or, if there are no numbers, about two-thirds of the way up).

Getting the levels right

Set a tune playing on one of the decks (or players or computer). Make sure the crossfader (the side-to-side slider in the middle) is set in the middle of its run. Turn on the corresponding channel on the mixer (if it has an on/off switch) and push the channel fader up to about halfway, or until the VU meters jump to somewhere in the middle without ever reaching into the red. Next, turn on the amp (and the monitor amp, if you have one) and slowly turn up the volume on the amp until you can hear the music at a pleasant level. It's usually not a good idea to crank up the volume until you have got everything up and running and have played a couple of tunes to confirm that everything is working as it should. Now you're ready to jam.

The Hamster Switch

As you will see from experimenting with the crossfader (the side-to-side slider), if you have a tune playing on both decks and the corresponding channel faders are pushed up far enough with the crossfader set in its middle, then you will be hearing both tunes at the same time. You can fade between channels by sliding the crossfader back and forth. This is the most

must know

If your mixer doesn't have a Hamster Switch, but you still want to mix the other way around, simply connect your right-hand deck to channel 1 and your left-hand deck to channel 2. The problem, of course, is that you would have to disconnect it all in the middle of your set to switch back.

basic way to mix between two records (more on this later).

Scratch DJs, however, are more demanding of their crossfaders than non-scratch mixers, who just use their crossfaders to fade smoothly between tunes. Scratchers need to alter the speed of the fade, fade very quickly and, occasionally, need to reverse it so that the sound fades in the other direction in order to perform certain tricks. For this purpose, many mixers have a sort of 'reverse' mode switch that, for reasons lost in the mists of club time, is known to all DJs as the 'Hamster Switch'.

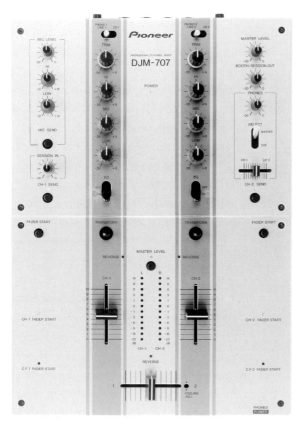

want to know more?
- Visit: http://www.djdown load.com for a wide selection of dance music
- Go to: http://www.beatport. com for the best dance catalogue in the world
- Check out: http://www.mixmag. net to learn about new tunes and re-releases

When not in use, the faders and all other switches on your mixer should be set in their neutral position - which is usually 'o'.

3 The first mix (drop mixing)

No more excuses. You know the essential gear and you know how to set it up and turn it on. In this chapter you'll learn the basic skills of handling and manipulating vinyl, CDs and digital controllers. It is also necessary, at this point, to learn a bit of proper music theory but – not to worry – it won't last long and it doesn't hurt. Most of what you need to know for drop mixing comes from a physical feel for the beat, the ability to count to four, a serious love of music and a large measure of patience. Get ready, it's time to learn how to DJ.

Handling vinyl records and CDs

You don't need to be a classically trained musician or have the hands of a surgeon, but it helps to understand which bits of a vinyl record do what. It also doesn't hurt to have a bit of dexterity and a good grip as you learn to use the tone arm.

must know

The darkest bits on a vinyl record, where the grooves are closer together, are the breakdowns where the music contains less information and a thinner groove was cut to store it. For a noisier part of the tune, place the needle on the lightest area.

Getting to know your vinyl

DJing is a physical art that requires intimate contact, so its a good idea for you and the record to get to know each other pretty well, pretty quickly. Start by choosing a piece of vinyl – not your favourite tune (since you are likely to damage it while learning) but one that you are quite fond of, as you are about to hear it around a thousand times.

After introducing yourself ('Hi, I'm DJ Novice'), examine your record closely on all sides and notice the different colours and textures which each tell you something about the music. The shiny smooth bits are the silences between songs, the darkest bits are the quiet sections and the gently-shaded slightly-shiny areas are likely to be the loudest bits. Rub your fingers over the record's surface until you can just about guess which is which and read it like Braille with your eyes closed. Practise holding the record only by its edges, placing it down on the platter, picking it up again and moving it to the other deck until you become adept enough to move swiftly and gracefully without ever leaving a fingerprint anywhere.

Remove the slipmat off one deck, place the tune on the platter and drop the needle. Watch the revolutions closely to see how well the platter's rubber top grips the vinyl. Practise lifting the tone arm back to its resting position, and then replacing it as closely as possible to the exact same spot on the vinyl. Keep practising this, using different target spots all over the record, until you develop a smooth action and feel comfortable with the tone arm's weight and delicacy. This is the easy part, so you need to be reasonably good at handling the tone arm before you move on.

If you make the odd mistake and end up scratching your record, don't worry about it. You will be glad you followed the advice on the opposite page and used an old record that is not a favourite. If you chose not to follow the advice, tough luck.

Always hold your vinyl records by their edges, as shown, and never touch the surface grooves unnecessarily.

Winding back and forward

Now it's time to work with sound coming through the speakers. With the slipmat back on, put the record on the deck, set it spinning with the arm on any tune and bring up the channel fader on the mixer for that deck.

must know

If the needle refuses to stick to the groove, check that the tonearm overhang, the weighting and the anti-skating are all set correctly. If it still won't stay, ensure the deck is level and stable and, lastly, that there isn't a load of fluff on the needle.

Checking the sound

Make sure that you can also play and hear a tune on the other deck by bringing up the other channel fader. Also, check that the crossfader fades between the two smoothly – and that all other controls, such as bass, middle and treble are set in the middle (or at 'o'), and that the main system sounds good. If you are in an enclosed DJ booth, remember that the sound is normally more bass-heavy and dull in these places, so step out onto the dancefloor to make sure it sounds good from there. It is always a good idea to have a clear sense of the way your mix is going to sound to the punters when the venue is full.

Starting to wind the vinyl

Start this exercise without sound by leaving the tone arm on its rest. Using a couple of right fingers, 'grab' the record in the middle of the grooves, on the opposite side of the vinyl to the tone arm, by pressing down on the vinyl. If you press hard enough – but not so hard that the platter underneath also stops – the record will stop spinning and will 'float' on the slipmat while the platter underneath continues to spin at full speed. While holding the vinyl, slowly move it a few inches forwards and

It takes a lot of practice to get it right, but it's crucial to master the art of smoothly 'winding' the record back and forth.

backwards and then hold it still again before finally letting go of it with a little 'push', so that it very quickly rides the platter again at full speed. Keep your movements smooth and fluid so that you do not damage the record or the needle as you push the record away.

When you feel reasonably comfortable with this physical handling of the vinyl with your fingers, put the tone arm down somewhere on the record and practise the above steps until you can start and stop the vinyl without making the tone arm jump – and without even making the stylus visibly vibrate. It's not easy and may take a while to get the hang of. But keep practising – for most people, the correct feel of the motion tends to 'click' after a few dozen attempts.

must know

Slipmats come in virtually every colour and pattern and you can even order your own design from various printing shops, though of course not many people will see it underneath the records you play.

Cueing

The first order of business in mixing is to find the 'cue point': the apparently invisible spot on the record from which you want to start your mix. The easiest-to-find cue point is always at the beginning of the record (the first beat of the first bar at the very beginning of the first song of the first side).

Finding the first beat

Set the record spinning and put the needle down right at the beginning, on the outer-most ring of lovely, shiny-smooth vinyl. When the music begins to play, 'grab' the record by stopping it physically (with a couple of fingers of either hand) just after you hear the first beat. While holding the record in place with your hand on the grooves, try a 'rewind' by moving your hand onto the label of the record. Do this quickly so as not to lose your place and with only one hand so that the other is free to work the mixer. With your first or second finger, wind the record anti-clockwise. Make sure you don't press too hard or the platter itself will stop – you only want the vinyl and the slipmat to stop. As you wind the record backwards, you will hear the tune play in reverse but keep going until you have passed the first beat (that is, until you hear silence). Now move your hand back onto the grooves (quickly again so as not to let the record move more than a couple of centimetres or so).

Wukka wukka

Now that you have apparently found the first beat, confirm this by slowly moving the vinyl forward slightly under the needle. When you hear the beginning of the sound, move it quickly backwards again to the silence

must know

Whenever you are learning a new move for a mix, try to keep an eye on the vinyl's paper label to note a reference point. As you become good at the move, it will always be even better if you can take your eyes off your hands and get your bearings just from the label out of the corner of your eye. This also allows you to pay attention to the other deck at the same time so as to prepare the next tune as far in advance as possible.

When you first hear that sweet 'wukka wukka' sound, you will know you are on your way to becoming a DJ.

before the first beat (and then forwards and backwards again many times). You should now be hearing that famous backwards-forwards sound known as 'wukka wukka'. When you feel comfortable with this move, try it while keeping your eyes on the label of the record in order to find a reference point for where the first beat is physically on the record. With practice, you might even be able to use that visual reference to find the beginning without listening (and when this happens you will know you are ultimately cool).

Now you need to learn to let go of the record each time so that it plays at the right speed immediately from the first beat. Keep your hand relaxed and try to feel the pull of the motor as you wukka-wukka over that first beat. Leave two centimetres or so before the first beat and relax your fingers as you give it a tiny push when you release it – but not so much as to make it go faster than the platter is already spinning underneath.

Music theory for DJs

The rhythm – the constant push – of every song is made up of evenly-spaced pulses called 'beats', which are the building blocks of music. Beats are not actual sounds, but rather are just the notional divisions in the music that never stop running.

Invisible structure

Beats do not depend on whether or not the drums are playing, and even a song without any drums at all will still have the same constant pulse made of the same beats as every other piece of music that has been written. To be sure, 'notes' are the sounds played by instruments while 'beats' are just the invisible structure of the music on which all music is based.

As a useful example, 'beats' are perhaps most easily identified (and can be simply found and counted out loud) in many classic House or Garage tunes where the bass drum thuds once for each beat of the bar. This is the easily-recognized '1-2-3-4' that dominates this style of music and is referred to as 'four-on-the-floor'.

1 Bar

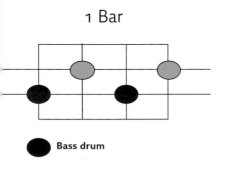

● **Bass drum**

● **Snare**

The diagram above demonstrates a standard bar or measure in popular music today in a typical House or Garage dance music tune.

Bars and measures

In most pop music (and in virtually all dance music), beats are organized into groups of four with each group of four called a 'bar' or 'measure'. Within each bar, the four beats have a regularly-occurring pattern in which the first and third beats are stronger 'downward' pulses while the second and fourth beats are the secondary 'upward' pulses, called 'off beats' or 'upbeats'. Almost without exception in dance music, the cracking snare drum marks the off beats on the second and fourth beat of each bar. The booming bass drum will almost always mark (at least) the first and third beats, which creates the easily recognizable 'boom–crack–boom–crack' as the sound of the 1-2-3-4 of each bar.

Hearing the beat

It's crucial for a DJ to hear the beats in all music straight away and, therefore, you should practise listening to records with this aim in mind. Try listening to any record – classic House or Garage tunes are recommended for this purpose – from somewhere in the middle of the tune and try to find the beat by tapping along with the bass drum (going 'boom-boom-boom-boom'). Notice that the snare drum 'cracks' on every other beat – these are the off beats, the snare playing with the bass drum on the second and fourth beat of each bar. Listen for a cymbal crash and, using this as a marker for the first beat of the bar, start counting from the cymbal as beat one. Without anyone else in the room – because it sounds so daft – practise counting aloud along with the song, checking for the big cymbal crashes that hit on beat one and the snare drum hits on beats two and four. To test yourself, start the record from a random spot and try to find the beginning of the bar (beat one) and count along with the tune, making sure that the snare drums hit on beats two and four. Try this with other tunes on the CD or with any records in your collection. Try to get comfortable with finding the beats, counting along and identifying the beginning of the bar as soon as possible after starting a new record.

Combinations

As we have seen, all music is made of notes (which are pitched high or low and may occur fast or slow) and beats (which run constantly in every song without stopping). Needless to say, DJs are primarily concerned with beats.

Bars and phrases

One easy way to get your head around all of this is to think of beats, the smallest division of music, as being the 'letters' in the alphabet and the bars as being the 'words' made up of the letters (usually four beats to a bar). The next largest division, being a group of bars, is called a 'phrase' (and, as the name implies, is a group of usually four, eight or sixteen bars, or 'words'). Phrases, being like musical sentences, tend to have recognizable beginnings and endings which, if you listen to the record a few times, become ever easier to spot and predict before they start and end. Now go back to the counting exercise above and try to identify the phrases in the record – remembering that phrases tend to start with a cymbal crash (or some obvious opening note) and tend to end as they fall in pitch or volume.

Some turntables feature a device which monitors tempo and BPM. This tells you that your record is playing at the correct speed.

Tempo and BPM

The speed, or 'tempo', of a tune is measured by the number of beats that go by in one minute and is therefore called its 'BPM' or 'Beats Per Minute'. It is actually possible to count the number of beats that go by in a tune during any 60 seconds to manually figure out the BPM. Luckily, this is seldom necessary, as the BPM of most Dance records – especially all extended dance mix singles – is written on the label, and, in the case of Dance MP3s, is often supplied with the file when you buy it. As a further convenience, some mixers actually have 'BPM counters' displayed in an LED screen – and computer mix programs always have huge BPM displays – which tell you the BPM of the record you are playing at that moment.

As we have seen, most music can be identified and grouped by its BPM: Reggae and Hip Hop are usually on the slower side (maybe 90–105 BPM) while House is at heartbeat speed in the middle (110–130 BPM) and Techno and Drum'n'Bass have the fastest tempos (135 BPM up to 200 BPM in some extreme cases). The whole concept of playing one record after another – and mixing two records together at the same time – is heavily dependent on the idea that they are at the same tempo, or can be made to play at the same tempo by adjusting one or both of the pitch controls. It is crucial, therefore, that every DJ develops a strong sense of hearing and feeling the beats, bars, phrases and tempo of a record deep inside himself or herself very instinctively. Not to worry, though: this is rarely a problem as most people naturally do this without being aware of it because, if they didn't, dancing itself would be impossible.

try this

If you are ever worried about the pace of a set, you can play the trick of starting the set at a quieter volume than normal and slowly raising the volume at the right points. Just be sure that you end up no louder than whatever maximum the sound system (and the club manager) will allow.

Fading, crossfading and segues

Once you have basically figured out what this music theory of beats and bars and tempo malarkey is all about, and have managed to actually master it in a few records, it is time to try putting it into practice. Go ahead, DJ.

Keeping it smooth

We have already seen how to put a tune on each deck and, by sliding up the channel fader for each deck and keeping the crossfader in the middle, listen to both tunes at the same time. So do this now and try to choose two tunes that are of the same genre, general feel and tempo.

As you probably know and have experienced, if the music ever stops on a dancefloor, even for a moment, most dancers quickly leave the floor for a drink, a smoke and a chat. Clearly, then, your job as a DJ is to make sure that, at all costs, the music never stops – not even for a split second – until you have finished your set or you need to go home or war breaks out, whichever is first. In short, your job is to provide a steady and constant stream of music, and it is the ingenious DJ mixer that allows you to do this. The various channel faders and the crossfader are designed to let you smoothly change decks and go from one record to another with no noticeable change in volume.

The crossfader is one cool tool that you will use constantly and throughout nearly every mix that you perform.

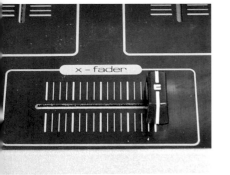

Fading

The faders on the mixer are primarily for adjusting the amount of sound that is sent from the source (the deck, player or computer) to the amplifier. There are two types of faders: the rotary fader, sometimes called a 'knob', which increases the level as you turn it, and the sliding fader that goes up in volume quite literally as it rises – but the latter sliding kind is far more common. Using the 'water' analogy we applied earlier, the fader is the 'tap', as it controls the amount of 'water' that is sent into the 'tank'. Clearly, it is important that, as with water, adjustments should be made slowly, a constant flow makes for the least mess, and – here's the crucial bit – as you slowly open one flow, then the other must be slowly closed so as to keep the overall amount at a constant flow.

Experiment with the volume levels on your mixer and you will soon master the basics of crossfading and creating segues.

Crossfading and segues

Coming back to actual DJing, set a tune playing on each of two decks and practice raising one level as you lower the other – trying always to keep the overall volume constant. When one fader is all the way down, the other should be all the way up – and vice versa – and when one fader is halfway up, the other should be at roughly the same position though there is a catch to this: when both of two faders are halfway up, the overall volume is not 'half of one and half of the other', as you would expect, but, rather, due to some weird kind of science, they both need to be slightly lower than halfway in order to add up to the same as a full fader of one or the other.

Once you get a feel for how the two faders interact and where they should sit to sound equal, try leaving both at a medium level and using the crossfader to fade between them.

This means of 'connecting' two tunes by fading between them without any loss in overall volume is called a 'segue' (pronounced 'seg-way') and forms the basis of all DJ mixing. Now you are ready to try proper drop mixing.

Drop mixing

Drop mixing is the name given to manually bringing in – that is, fading in – a new record (and fading out the old one) so smoothly that the mix does not miss a beat.

Picking a suitable tune

The trick requires that you master the manual dexterity of cueing the new record properly and the art of fading the faders properly, though all the skill and agility in the world will not help if you try to drop mix to an entirely unsuitable record: a slow ballad will almost never work butted-up against a HiNRG Drum'n'Bass tune. Therefore, for these early attempts at drop mixing, use two tunes that are so close in tempo, style and feel as to be nearly two mixes of the same tune. In fact, to make things easy on yourself, use two mixes of the same tune (if not two copies of the same record).

Practise drop mixing at home or in a DJ booth on your own before you give it a go in your set.

Preparing the mix

As the first tune is playing away on the first deck, begin by finding the first beat of the track you are going to mix to, much as you did at the beginning of this chapter, but this time use the 'monitor' function of your mixer so that you hear it only in the headphones. This is very important, of course, because the audience needs to be hearing and dancing to only the first tune while you cue up and prepare the mix. Most mixers have a 'PFL' (Pre Fader Listen) switch for each channel that, when pressed, lets you listen to that channel's deck on the headphones. If this doesn't work, it's usually because either you haven't brought the channel fader up (with the crossfader to the opposite side to keep that deck out of the main mix and the main speakers) or the master volume level for the 'monitor' or 'PFL' function is not up high enough. If it still doesn't work, your headphones aren't working (or are not plugged in), or you need to consult the mixer's manual.

Let's review the cueing procedure (and simplify it a bit this time):

- Find a reasonably suitable 'out point' on the first record, which will be the moment in that first record at which the old record fades out and the new record comes in. The end of a big phrase or section will usually do. When you finally choose your 'out point', start that first record again from a spot about one minute before the 'out point'. This will give you enough time to do the rest of the instructions below before that 'out point' comes up (if you don't make it in time, you'll need to quickly choose a later 'out point' or start the whole exercise again).

- Remember that you need always to keep the first record playing in the speakers to the dancefloor while you are doing the instructions below (while listening only on headphones to the new record).

- Set the new record playing right from the start, but quickly catch it and wind back to the first beat (that is, place a finger on the centre label and rewind it back briskly, anticlockwise, with the needle on the record). Once you hear the telltale 'end' of the sound, which is actually the first beat of the song, wind the record back one whole revolution further. This will give you time to move your hand to a comfortable position for manipulating the record before the first beat plays. If one whole revolution is not enough, try one and a half, or two.

- Remember that the cueing up of the new record is done while keeping the platter running – so you will need to ensure that the slipmat is slippy enough to let you move the record around and then hold it still without losing your place.

- As the first record is playing away and approaching your chosen 'out point', and you are holding the new record still just before the first beat of the first song (the 'in point' or 'cue point'), you now have to concentrate harder than you have ever concentrated before. It takes even more concentration than that 'rub your tummy and pat your head' thing. The trick is to return your musical mind back to the first record, figure out where you are in it, and starting counting backwards as a countdown to the 'out point'.

- As you are nearing the 'out point' – probably about one or two beats before the actual 'out point' – you need to let go of the new record, or give it a little push, so that it starts on its first beat at just the moment the new record reaches the 'out point'. Finally, as one last challenge, you need also to move the crossfader over so that the new record is heard instead of the old one.

- Obviously it doesn't work the first time you try it. Or the second or third. But keep practising – it will come good in the end.

- Bob is your uncle.

Once you have cued up the first track on the new record, hold the record in place as you prepare to bring it in with the crossfader.

My first mix

Well, that's it – if you have followed the advice of the preceding pages, you should be beginning to successfully mix records. However, there are a few things to remember...

Your first mix checklist

- Always make sure that the overall speed switch is set to the correct choice of either 33 RPM or 45 RPM ('revolutions per minute'). 99.9 per cent of the time you will want 33 RPM, but there are a few wacky singles out there that still use the faster speed.

- If you simply let go of the new record, the sound will speed up over the first couple of bars, as the slipmat catches up with the platter. Instead you

Check you have set the deck at the correct speed for the tune and, if you haven't played it for a while, check if it needs a quick wipe for dust.

Practise pushing the second record until you develop a smooth action, as opposed to an uncontrolled flick.

need to give the record a gentle push as you release it. Position your wrist roughly over the centre of the record so that you can use it as a pivot. Try to keep your fingers relaxed and supple so that you can feel the speed that the platter wants to move at, and ease the record forward as your fingers unfurl rather than flicking the record onwards sharply, which would make it harder to control. Practise these steps until you can consistently bring in the record at its proper full tempo from the start.

• Make sure both channel faders are set at the same level so that when you throw the crossfader over the volume stays the same between the two records – if you are mixing two quite different

The key to effective drop mixing is to ensure that the second record falls in sync with the first so that the steady beat is never lost.

records, you might need to have one fader slightly lower than the other to achieve the consistent volume across the drop mix of the two records.

• The aim of the drop mix is to set the new record running just before the correct beat so that the new record falls in time with the old. If the start point of the new record is the first beat of the song (or of a phrase), then wait until the end of a similar sort of phrase in the old record to use as the 'out point'. Ideally, with good timing of your hands and a smooth crossfade, the first beat on the new record should feel like the first beat of the next phrase in the old record.

- If you have chosen an 'off beat' (that is, a 2 or a 4) as an 'out point' then, similarly, you will need to replace it with an offbeat from the new record. This can be effective, but it is pretty difficult to do and should not be attempted too early in your learning curve.

- When you are dropping in the first beat of a new phrase, you may find it is helpful to do a simple rhythmic 'scratch' on the 1-2-3-4 in the last bar of the phrase before the 'out point', to help you feel where the beat falls. Bring the new record forward over the first beat (which is usually a bass drum (or 'kick drum') and then backwards again in time to move the record forward again on the next beat. This produces the classic 'wukka wukka' sound (see pages 52–3) before the beat drops in so, aside from probably being quite helpful to your drop mixing education, it also sounds wicked.

want to know more?
- Visit your local music shop to try out different kinds of gear
- Visit: www.pointblanklondon .com for useful DJ information
- Visit: http://www.clubdjzone .com for DJ forums and networks

To produce an effective drop mix, it is vital to position your stylus correctly to ensure it does not get bumped or knocked.

4 Basic DJing techniques (beat mixing)

Let's get straight to the heavy stuff: two turntables and two kickin' tunes – what else could a person want? Well, an ability to beat mix, for a start. Drop mixing is an important skill to learn, to be sure, but if that is all you can do, you might as well work the back corner of the bar down at the Holiday Inn on Mother's Day. It's mixing, Jim, but not as we know it. Now beat mixing, well, that is mixing. You need to learn a bit more music, and the moves can be tricky to master, but in the end this is the stuff of happiness and dreams. And proper DJing.

Tempo and speed

This is where you begin to hear yourself making cool sounds and becoming a DJ. But this is also where the work starts. No pain, no gain. And no giving up, please.

'Train' theory

Beat mixing is the art of synchronizing two tunes so perfectly as to create the effect that only one tune is playing. This allows the DJ to overlap the two records (for a few bars usually) when mixing from one to the next in the mix. This is also the magical method by which a DJ can spontaneously create a 'new' record out of two existing ones, right before the audience's very eyes and ears by playing one record over another most of the way through. However, in order for beat mixing not to sound like a car crash, the two records must keep perfect time and their sounds, beats and music must all blend together well enough to make a third, new record.

In short, beat mixing is achieved by the DJ adjusting the speed of one of the records so that it runs 'in synch' with the other either by hand or by using the pitch control. Both methods, remember, are nothing more than just ways to keep two records running at the same speed. Speed is the key thing here and it is crucial to understand exactly what this means.

Unfortunately, for reasons related to faulty manufacturing, inconsistent power supplies or warped vinyl, even if you try to beat mix two copies of the same record, they will still run at slightly different speeds and tempos and you will still have to use your skill to make them run at exactly the same speed in order to stay in synch.

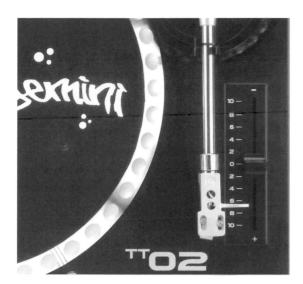

The pitch control on your turntable can be used for fine-tuning the speed at which your records play.

To make two records run at the same speed, imagine two railway trains trying to drive together in the same direction down their tracks side-by-side. No matter how hard the drivers try to drive at the same speed, sooner or later one train will go slightly faster or slightly slower than the other, because few machines, and fewer humans, are perfect. The first trick is to figure out which train is speeding up or slowing down. Think of sitting in a train while looking out of the window and seeing another train go slowly past the window. Is your train going slower and letting the other train pass? Or is the other train speeding up and passing you? As train passengers know very well, it's impossible to tell without some kind of reference mark for you to get your bearings.

The need for speed

It is quite impossible to bring both trains level (by speeding up or slowing down) until you know

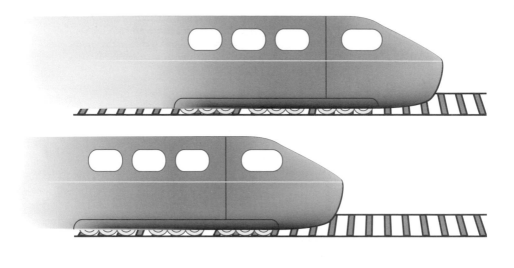

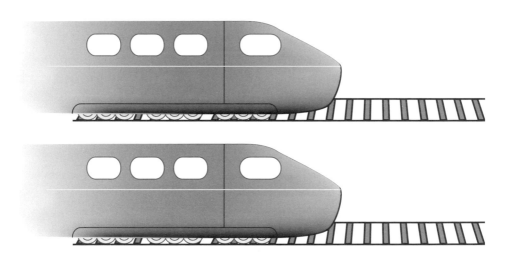

Synchronizing the beats of two records is like trying to get two trains running side-by-side at exactly the same speed. In the diagram above, the first train is running faster than the second (top). If the first train slows down momentarily to wait for the second train, they can both run together evenly (bottom).

Some turntables feature more
advanced pitch controls, with
digital LED screens.

which one is doing what. If the other train is
slightly ahead of yours but going at exactly the
same speed, then it will stay just ahead without
seeming to move. In that case, you'll have to speed
up your train for just a short moment until it
becomes level with the other and then slow down
again to match its speed. Or it could slow down for
a moment to let you catch up and then speed up
again to stay level.

Beat mixing two records is very much the same
sort of thing. You need to start by deciding which
record is ahead or behind – or going too fast or too
slow – and then (and only then) you need to correct
the problem by doing the opposite thing to that
record until the problem is corrected and the records
are again even and going at exactly the same speed.
And, the trouble is, you have to keep doing this act of
'decision/correction' constantly while the two
records are running together.

Beat mixing

As with drop mixing, beat mixing depends on spotting compatible phrases in records. When you think you've found two similar records, put them to the acid test on opposite decks and listen to them one right after the other.

must know

There are certain points in each tune that are best for mixing out. House tunes, for instance, tend to start with solo drum beats for easy mixing in and breakdowns tend to have moments of high impact that are ideal for mixing in or out.

The basics

As you listen to the two similar records, one straight after the other, try to spot the differences: is one at a faster tempo than the other? Are their phrases of different length? Also, try to spot the similarities: are all the phrases in each of the records the same length – or do they change? Are there any false starts or tricky bits that interrupt phrases? These sorts of decisions about differences and similarities are the meat and potatoes of beat mixing. Once you find two suitable records which are very nearly the same tempo (for a simple solution, use two mixes – or even two copies – of the same tune), cue them up and let's get it on.

Begin by drop mixing each one from the beginning and try to guess which is going faster or slower. This is a good moment to practise your drop mixing again, so try starting the first tune from the beginning and mix in the next tune at exactly the first beat of the second phrase of the first record. Choose specific points and practise drop mixing until you can pinpoint any spot and drop the second record in on target.

To begin your first beat mix, make sure both pitch controls are at 'o' and cue both tunes up to where the drums start (hopefully, both at the beginning of

To slow the record down, gently brush the edge of the vinyl with your finger, applying more or less pressure as necessary.

the record). You have to start your beat mix with a good drop mix so that both records start in synch at the right time and then you can think about which one is pulling ahead or falling behind. The quicker they fall out of time, the bigger the difference in tempo between the two records and the more you will have to adjust the speed of one of them.

Manual pitch shifting to slow down

After listening to the two records run together for a few bars, decide which one is running faster than the other. Let your finger or thumb brush against the side of that record platter for an instant. The more pressure you apply, or the longer you apply it, the more it will slow down.

Push down on the record in a clockwise direction to speed up the rate at which it is playing.

Another method is to gradually and gently squeeze the spindle at the centre of the turntable for just a short moment. This will slow it down, but has a more subtle effect.

Manual pitch shifting to speed up

For maximum control, put your finger on the label of the record and push downwards into the platter to disable the slipmat. Then, move the record onwards slightly faster in a clockwise direction, taking care to keep applying the pressure downwards as well as in a circular motion. For smaller adjustments, turn the spindle faster or physically (but very gently) push the record onwards clockwise (but not the platter itself).

Once you have managed to bring the two into synch, you will probably notice that they fall out again rather quickly. Try again to guess which record is going faster or slower and again make a small adjustment on the pitch control in the opposite way; for example, if record 2 is going too fast, pull down its

pitch control a little bit. Now decide which record is doing what and repeat the whole thing again. By doing this over and over again you will continue to make the problem smaller and smaller – and eventually unnoticeable.

Using these techniques, it is possible to bring the two records nearly exactly into synch with each other and to keep them there. Sometimes, when the two copies of the same record are running perfectly together, you will hear them 'phase' (a freaky psychedelic side-effect – more on this later).

While you're practising , mostly leave the crossfader in the middle to hear both records in the speakers. However, in order to simulate a real performance, do your beat mixing with the first record in the speakers and the one that you're adjusting only in the headphones; when you finally get both records running at the same speed, that's when you throw the crossfader to the middle so that the crowd can hear both at the same time.

If the records fall out of synch, pull down the pitch control or simply hold one of them back a little until you can match them up correctly once more.

Phrase matching

Now that you know how to BPM-match two records, you need to 'phrase match' them for a perfect beat mix. This is tougher, but with practice you will soon get the hang of it.

Keeping your phrases in line

Even when two records are running at the same speed, the switch from one to the other will not be smooth if, say, the first record is playing at 1-2-3-4 as the second record is playing 2-3-4-1. In other words, both records always have to be BPMed and be lined-up so that the bars match beat-for-beat as they run. Like the train passenger hoping to see their friend in the next train, the two trains must run at the same speed, but they must also have the right windows aligned next to each other.

As usual, start by BPM-matching the two tunes and then drop mix one into the other so that the 'in point' and 'out point' create perfectly aligned phrases. Remembering that fine-tune adjustments to speed will be constantly necessary to counter-act the inevitable slight changes in speed, try to keep the phrases aligned for as long as possible. You will quickly notice that it is crucial to regularly make very small and quite quick speed adjustments so as to not let one record speed up or slow down enough to fall out of phrase alignment. When you finally manage to get both running together like identical twin trains, you can then fade or quickly switch between them without the audience hearing any difference in speed or phrase and, as if by magic, they will think the whole mix is just one very groovy, seamless and ultimately danceable record.

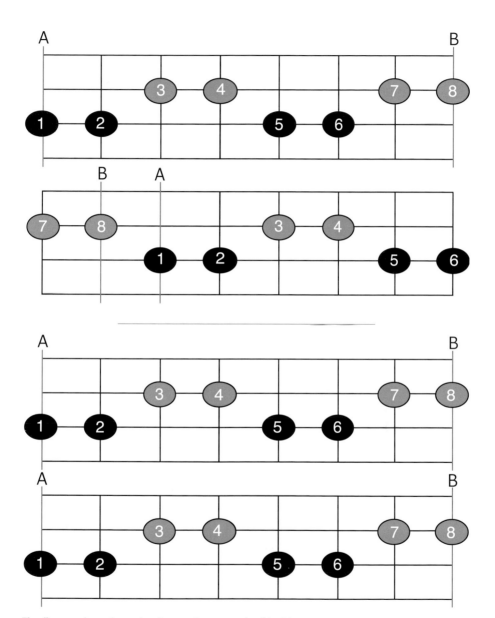

The diagram above shows the phrases of two records with eight beats, starting at A and finishing at B. In the first example (top) the second phrase starts two beats too late. To match the phrases, both need to start on the first beat (A) at the same time (bottom).

Synchronization

Time to put it all together and create a slamming beat mix. Perfect synchronization of all your different elements is the key to success. Let's get it on.

Everything in line

Start record 1 with the crossfader all the way to its side and cue up record 2 (using the headphones on 'monitor' or 'PFL', of course). Hold record 2 on the slipmat (over the spinning platter) just before the first beat of the cue point, ready to spin it in. Lift one side of your headphones so that you can hear record 1 on the main speakers. Find your beat and place in record 1 (tap your foot in time, for maximum groove with record 1). Next, rock record 2 back and forth in time to record 1, creating the wukka wukka 'scratch' sound with the first beat of the cue point on record 2. Count along with record 1 (1–2–3–4, 2–2–3–4, 3–2–3–4, 4–2–3–4) until it gets to the 8th bar (8–2–3–4). Then, on that last '4', release record 2 with a gentle push and keep gently pushing it until the beats match. They are likely to stay in synch for only one or two

When you are cueing up record 2, listen for the beat with your cans set to 'monitor' or 'PFL'.

bars, so try as quickly as possible to guess whether record 2 is going too fast or too slow. Now put the headphones back on to both ears for a second and take one ear off again to re-check record 2 against record 1. Is it too fast or too slow? If record 2 feels like its racing ahead, slow it down a bit with a small and quick move. If record 2 feels lazy, give a sharp quick surge fast-forward. Keep adjusting in this way until the beats again match perfectly. Keep your index finger on the spindle (the centre of the record) and keep winding it up to increase speed or faintly brush the outer edge of the vinyl for a split second to slow it down. Keep adjusting the pitch control as necessary – whatever it takes – to keep the two trains running evenly.

Perfecting the technique

When you have comfortably achieved an even speed and the two records are running in perfect phrase alignment, start playing with the crossfader, performing slow and quick crossfades in both directions and on or off the beat. Ensure the channel faders are set appropriately so that the volume of both records sounds the same (or adjust one or other of the channel faders accordingly).

The most useful sound for checking perfect beat matching is usually the kick drum, which will add a 'clatter' to the combined sound of the two records if the match is not perfect. For very fine-tuning of your beat mix, select PFL for both channels at the same time and adjust the speeds until that clatter is gone and the kick drums together sound like one drum. This should indicate that you have achieved perfection and usually means it is time to get jiggy with both tunes loud on the main speakers.

watch out!

If you intend to mix two full-vocal tunes, be sure to avoid playing the vocal passages of each record together. Also try to avoid cutting out or bringing in a tune mid-vocal by waiting for a gap in the singing or at the natural end of a phrase.

Blending and cutting

The moment you choose to throw over the crossfader from record 1 to record 2 (or vice versa) will make or break your mix. Obviously, as a good listener, you will have begun by choosing the beginnings and ends of phrases as your mix points, and that is no bad thing. But now you need to take it further...

Know your records

As we have seen, the trick in finding 'in points' and 'out points' is to count the bars of record 1, while also being aware of where you are in record 2 and vice versa. The process is a lot easier, of course, if you know your records very well. If you're certain of when record 1 will hit a breakdown, then it's infinitely easier to mix into it at exactly the right moment. This is especially exciting and effective with well-known records, as you can surprise the dancefloor by mixing in or out of a tune at precisely the moment they expect something quite different. It's all about trial and error, practice and knowing your tunes like the back of your hand.

Choose any two tunes and you will find they have certain phrases and sections that could never beat mix together well. Some helpful rules for selecting tunes to beat mix:

- Never beat mix two vocals. If you mix a vocal at all, remember to mix in and out at the beginning and end of the phrase so that the vocal doesn't seem to fade in or out unnaturally when you mix in and out.
- Never beat mix two chunky or pumping basslines, as the result is always just too big.

- Never beat mix two tunes of wildly different tempos, as the required pitch change will probably be too far.
- Drums-only sections usually work together best, but those which are particularly busy tend to sound messy when combined.
- As far as possible, try the tunes together at home first.
- Always know your records well.

When switching the cross-fader onto the new record, gently push the record forwards with your hand.

Using the pitch control

After you become comfortable with beat mixing two tunes that are very close in tempo, you'll be ready to start again with records of more varied tempos. However, because manual changes will not suffice for large differences in tempo, you will need to use the pitch controls.

Numark decks feature pitch controls with a digital readout.

What do they do?

The pitch controls of most decks will speed up or slow down a record by up to about eight per cent but unfortunately and annoyingly, as the tempo (and speed) increases, so does the pitch. Remember that a track played at a much faster speed than normal will probably sound like Mickey Mouse on helium, and a record played too slowly will usually sound lazy and drunk.

For this more difficult beat mix, start by drop mixing the two tunes from the beginnings of phrases that are not too radically different (or, at least, have similar drum patterns). Decide whether the second track is going faster or slower: are the beats racing ahead and reaching the end of the phrase too quickly? Or are they falling behind and dragging? Try listening to the same instrument in the two tunes together – kick drums, high hats and snares often work well for these purposes. When you've decided which is which, use the pitch control to make one deck go faster or slower. You'll have to use the pitch control quite vigorously to simulate the movements that you were doing manually in the easier beat mix. You will probably need to temporarily over-compensate if a deck is going too slowly by throwing the pitch control up quite high for just a moment and then jerking it back down quickly with your hand. Remember that if one record is at a faster tempo than the other, the pitch control for that deck will have to remain lower than 'o' for most of the mix – and occasionally you may have to pull it even lower to bring it into synch before then returning the control to its less-than-zero position for the two to run consistently together.

Over-compensating

The key point is that you must continually over-compensate for each change in speed. If you suddenly have to speed up record 1 to make it catch up with record 2, you would then wait until record 1 not only reached the correct tempo but was beginning to push ahead of record 2. You would then slow down record 1 again to just below what you thought was the real tempo of the record (say, about minus 1.5 per cent on the pitch control) for a short moment. Finally you would speed record 1 up again to, say, plus two per cent (or whatever was the real speed) only when you had successfully counter-acted the original over-acceleration. So, using this method, the DJ is constantly pushing the pitch control up and down but always returning to some point in the middle (which isn't 'o', but is some point which is the higher or lower speed that matches record 2).

Of course, in practice most DJs will use both the manual and pitch control methods together at all times to beat mix.

did you know?

The term 'pitch control' is most-often used for fine-tuning the speed of the motor on a deck, while the term 'vari-speed' is usually used in relation to tape machines – on which the voltage is varied to make the tape machine play slower or faster.

Mixing out and matching levels

Once you have beat matched the tunes, remember also to make the phrases of the two tunes move from one to the other as naturally as possible – which suggests that a beat mix of less than eight bars will rarely work.

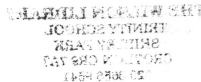

The simple method

The easiest way to bring a new record into the mix is at the beginning of a phrase, by bringing the crossfader to the centre on the first beat and then quickly completing the journey of the crossfader to the other side. Likewise, to fade out of the mix, try to fall into the new tune on the first beat of a phrase.

Matching levels

At all times when beat mixing, try to ensure that both records are at equal volume so there is no perceptible change in the overall volume when mixing between them. More crucially, never give in to the temptation to bring in a new record louder than the previous one, as it would soon leave you stranded with nowhere to go (and, besides, it should be you that rocks the crowd, not the volume).

A sharp rise in levels from one record to another will usually break the continuity of the mix (though sometimes a big jump can be a useful effect).

The crossfader is designed when moving from side to side to keep the overall volume constant. Remember that the level often rises a tiny bit, however, when you move to the hard left or hard right – because there is only one record in the mix at those points, rather than the two records that share the mix when the crossfader is anywhere in the middle.

In the unlikely event that your mixer has no crossfader (and even if it does, many DJs prefer this method), you

should get used to constantly adjusting the volumes on the channel faders, as development of this skill and instinct offers extra possibilities in your mixing. When you bring in record 2 in a beat mix, try to introduce it at a slightly lower level while leaving the first track at full volume. As you start to switch over to it, any rise in record 2 must be matched by a drop in the first one. Adjust both at the same time to keep a constant volume.

To compare the levels of the two tunes (at home), play a record on each turntable – without beat mixing – and see which one sounds louder when the channel fader is at the same height. When you notice a louder one you'll know this channel fader must always be set a bit lower for that record (and make a note of this on the sleeve or label).

Now, with the crossfader all the way over to one side, beat match the record on the other deck in the headphones only. When you get them matched, cue the second tune up and set it running from a spot 8 or 16 bars before the point where you want to beat mix the two. Just as that spot comes, throw the crossfader over and listen to how they sound together. If it sounds good, keep them both in for a while. If not, get the crossfader over quickly to get yourself out as fast as possible.

Listen to the crowd's reaction to your mix and never, ever, bring both faders to the top at the same time, or you could blow the sound system.

want to know more?

- The DJ school at www.pointblanklondon.com features DJ lessons online.
- Visit: www.crossfader.com, an 'online community for the global electronic artist' and an interesting site for turntablists.
- See: http://www.beatmixing.com for further tips on beat mixing.

5 Advanced DJing techniques

You know the equipment, you're a vinyl junkie, you've got the gear and you've got the basic skills. But there's more: the style and panache of the best DJs comes not only from the ability to mix without falling, but also from the spices and flavours that turn a standard set – even of awesome tunes – into a unique musical performance. A good crowd will, understandably, expect the DJ to create something new, different and original at every gig. Arise, Sir Disc Jockey.

Panning

The learning curve from here on in is very steep. Don't expect to master panning or the following skills overnight and try not to let yourself get discouraged by initial failures. Hang in there, though: the feeling you get when it finally works is worth all the pain. You will make it in the end – just keep going.

Pan settings

The 'panning' knob, usually found above the channel fader for each channel on a mixer, is intended to move the sound from one speaker to the other, so as to take advantage of a 'stereo' sound system. When set in the middle position, it sends an equal level of the sound in that channel to each speaker.

While pan settings in a home or studio sound system can create dramatic depth and space to the music, any setting of the pan control other than dead centre should generally be avoided in a club or other big room system. If, for instance, the vocals were panned to the right and the drums to the left, you might easily find that the people standing near the door have no beat to dance to and the people at the other side are bored by the instrumental tunes. For this reason, most club systems are set up as 'mono' systems in which no difference can be made to what comes out of each speaker. In this case, panning a channel might simply make the sound in that channel softer (or it might make no difference at all). In bigger clubs, therefore, it is always best to ensure that all the pans are set to the middle before you begin your set.

Panning effects

In smaller clubs, however, if the sound system is set up to allow it, panning of certain sounds can create useful and cool effects. One dramatic effect is to slowly pan from left to right and back again a non-drums record (a vocal or a breakdown section with vocals or a solo instrument, for instance), over the top of a grooving record. The sweeping effect can often make an entire audience sway with the movement. If you do choose to pan drum sounds, try quick pans to make the individual drum hits ricochet around the room. This can be very effective.

Panning effects can be a useful tool in smaller clubs, but they take a lot of practice to get right.

A cappella mixing

Mixing an a cappella vocal (that is, a vocal on its own without any accompaniment or other sounds at all) over another tune is much the same as doing a conventional running mix, but with a few key differences and requirements to keep in mind.

The rules of good a cappella

- Choose the record you mix the vocal over very carefully. If the vocal is out of tune with the track underneath, it is probably going to sound a bit weird (if not disastrously awful). On the other hand, a mix that cleverly puts a vocal into an interesting and new musical context can send the dancefloor crazy. It may even be a basis for creating a proper new record in the recording studio – this was the case for *You Got the Love* by The Source featuring Candi Staton, which originally was a bootleg of the Candi Staton a cappella over the Frankie Knuckles instrumental *Your Love*.

- Most vocals do not start on the first beat of the bar. Study the a cappella carefully to figure out what beat the first word should be on.

- If you have to change the speed (manually or with the pitch control) of an a cappella during a mix, try to do so in the silent bits between words so that no one hears the changes in pitch and speed, as this often makes the vocal sound mangled and sick. In an emergency, try changing it during a loud drum bit on the other record where the change will be less noticeable.

- It is much harder to be as precise with tempos on a cappellas as there are no obvious drum beats to mix to. If you have to slow down or speed up dramatically, use the 'over-compensation' technique and stick to silent moments for the biggest changes. On the other hand, a cappellas can be quite forgiving to less-than-perfect beat mixing, as there will be no clattering of out-of-synch drums or other instruments.

- When a groove in a vocal exists, find it and mix to it as much as possible.

A cappella mixes can be the coolest and most useful tool in a DJ's arsenal.

Tone and frequency

Here's a bit of serious science for you: sound actually moves through the air in much the same way as a wave of water moves through the sea. Even though air is invisible, it moves through the air in waves of varying size that literally 'hit' our ear, enabling us to hear the sound that they carry.

must know

The frequency range of music (and of the human ear) starts with the lowest-possible pitch at 20 Hertz and extends to the very highest-pitched sounds at 20,000 Hertz. In reality, however, most people's ears cannot reach these extremes and more likely can only hear from about 50 Hertz to about 14,000 Hertz. The human with the widest range and best sense of hearing is statistically most likely to be a five-year-old girl. This is because babies are born without the ear fully developed, the ears begin to deteriorate at about the age of six, and in any case females tend to have better hearing than males.

Sound waves and frequencies

Sound waves that we hear can be as big as four metres or as short as a few centimetres. Sound waves, like water waves, travel by 'swimming' through the air in an alternating up-then-down motion and the length of each full up-then-down motion determines the 'frequency' of that wave and, therefore, the pitch of its sound. Big and long waves make low bass sounds, while small and short waves make high-pitched sounds.

Human ears can hear a wide range of frequencies, extending from the low rumble of a volcano to the high whine of a television. In numbers, the human ear can hear the range of 20 Hertz (or 'Hz'), which in music would be the lowest thud of a deep Reggae bass, all the way up to 20,000 Hertz (or '20'kHz'), which would be the highest airy sound of a piccolo. Most sounds use a range of these 'frequencies', so it should be remembered that even the low bass has some sounds as high as maybe 1,000 Hz, while the piccolo may have some part of its sound as low as 21 or 23,000 Hz.

How EQ works

The function of an equalizer (or 'EQ') is to add or subtract parts of a sound either to cure some problem (such as to remove a background hiss or a low rumble) or to make some sound seem different in some way (such as to give a human voice more clarity or to give a bass drum more 'oomph').

An EQ has two main sets of controls: one to select the range that you wish to affect (usually treble, mid-range and bass) and one to affect that chosen range(s) (usually to add or subtract some amount of that range). The classic EQ knobs roughly equate as follows: bass = 100 Hz, mid-range = 1000 Hz, and treble = 10kHz. Some mixers have a third set of controls which affect the 'bandwidth' or the amount of each range to be changed. These equalizers are known as 'parametric EQ' and are found only on top-of-the-range gear. If you ever have the privilege of using one, start with a medium setting for the bandwidth and experiment outwards in both directions.

EQ settings

The most basic kind of EQ is known as the 'graphic EQ' and is easily recognized by the many rows of sliders, each labelled with a frequency. As most HiFi users know, the left-hand sliders boost the bass when pushed up and cut the bass when pushed down, while the right-hand ones similarly affect the higher sounds. On expensive rigs, these graphic EQs may have 30 or more individual sliders to play with (and will provide hours of experimental fun to the first-timer).

In general, DJs should be very careful when setting these EQs, the main worry being that the sound may be radically different in each part of the room. The corners of a room are notorious for 'trapping bass' – a cool expression which means that the bass sounds bounce back and forth between surfaces (such as adjacent parallel walls in corners) causing the music to sound muddy and boomy. The open middle of any room will usually sound better than the areas near the walls and corners. This is because the speakers normally face out into the middle and listeners in their direct path will hear them as they are intended to be heard (without reflections and interference from walls). However, it is always possible that the odd column in the middle of a room may sometimes adversely affect the quality of sound.

Reference records

It is also crucial that you choose a 'reference record' to use when checking out a room, so that you have something to compare it with. Ideally you should select a record that you love and know very well and ensure that you always use the

Most mixers come equipped with basic EQ settings for high, mid and low frequencies.

More advanced mixing desks allow you to adjust virtually every aspect of your sound.

same copy of that tune in every situation. Try to develop your own standards and vocabulary to judge the sound of your reference record, using criteria such as 'boomy in the middle 8 section', 'bright and clear vocals' or 'hits you in the gut on the first beat of the chorus', and in each case in every different new room listen to see if these factors are the same (or if they occur) in various parts of the room.

In this way, you should be able to identify the deficiencies of the room and try to compensate with a variety of fix-its.

It is always worth getting a second person to assist with EQ settings, to adjust the gear while you move around listening, and to provide an extra opinion. The first fix to try in every case is a change in the position or direction of the speakers – the slightest twist in the direction a speaker is facing can sometimes make a huge

watch out!
Even when two records drop mix together nicely in tempo and feel, they might still jar if they have different overall tone and sound quality, and a slight adjustment in EQ often helps. If the new tune is too tinny or weak, boost the bass a bit. If it's too boomy, turn down the bass a bit.

Recording consoles often boast highly sophisticated EQ controls for very fine adjustments.

difference to its sound – or, if the speakers are bolted down or otherwise impossible to move, some careful and sparing use of sophisticated EQ. When you do begin trying to adjust the EQ, start with very small changes and try to notice the difference. Continue with this incremental process by adding or subtracting a similarly-small amount and checking out the new sound until you have compensated just enough for the problem you first identified. Try not to go on making further changes based on the newly-adjusted sound, as this can easily get out of control and end up with a wildly-adjusted awful-sounding system that was, inevitably, better before you started fiddling. Indeed, if you should ever suspect for one second that it was better in the first place, then by all means go with your instinct and undo your mad changes.

Sound checks

Also remember that whatever you do during the sound check in the afternoon is likely to be different during your set at night. Firstly, this is because most people have a tendency to play their set with slightly more volume than they had planned and, secondly, because the presence of hundreds of writhing, sweaty humans is also likely to alter the sound. If the room is big and open-plan, the dancing bodies are likely to make your set sound bassy and boomy while the same people in a room with loads of nooks and crannies will most likely make the sound light and tinny. The only way to deal with this problem is in hindsight – by going on a crowded night to hear someone else's set – and of course hindsight is a luxury that cannot always be planned for, so the safest plan is just to assume the sound will be muddier on the night and take that into account during your afternoon listening session.

Sound checks are important for obvious reasons, but allow for the fact that when the room is full of dancers, the sound of your system will likely change.

As a golden rule when trying to EQ someone else's system, always write down on paper the existing settings before you change anything so that you can return it all to the owner's preferred settings when your set is done. If you have no pen or paper, or cannot see the settings well enough to mark them with reasonable accuracy, it is best not to touch and just leave things as they are.

High-pass and low-pass filters

Many mixers feature a high-pass filter ('HPF') and/or a low-pass filter ('LPF') on each channel. The most confusing thing about these otherwise simple devices is that the HPF allows only low-pitched sounds to get through (so it cuts away the treble) and the LPF allows only high-pitched sounds to get through (so it cuts away the bass). An HPF can be useful if the system is too brittle or toppy, while the LPF is probably most useful when a system has a low-hum feedback problem. Be very careful with these knobs, however, as even minimal use can easily cause your system to sound weak (with no bass) and/or sound muffled (with no treble). Remember the rule for EQ: if in doubt, leave it out.

Using EQ in your set

As we have seen, EQ can be used to correct deficiencies of the room or the system, but depending on the sort of EQ you have on your mixer, it can also be used to enhance a particular tune or aspect of your mix. Assuming your mixer has at least the basic three knobs for treble, mid and bass for each channel (and if it doesn't, you

must know

Every beat of every tune of every kind of music in the world can always be divided into two smaller halves, which themselves can be divided again until the divisions are too small and too fast to hear.

should consider upgrading), there are several tricks that you can use to assist your mix.

The most basic, and often most helpful, manoeuvre is to cut the bass by twisting the bass adjustment knob on the relevant channel counter-clockwise as far as it goes. This can be a life-saving move when a mix is going wrong, because the clatter that occurs when two records are fighting each other while the crossfader is in the middle and the tunes are sharing the speakers usually sounds far less messy if the big low bass sounds are removed (i.e. one bass drum is better than two unmatched bass drums). Usually, when performing a bass cut on an EQ, you will want to turn the knob down very quickly just before the first beat of a bar. Then, turn it back to the middle 'o' position just as quickly and also just before the first beat of a bar. This makes it sound like the EQ effect was intended on the record. However, if you're in a bind during a crossfader move, sometimes you just have to bite the bullet and twist away willy-nilly. A badly-performed effect is always less damaging than a badly-botched changeover – especially if you can avoid making the crowd lose the groove.

Alternative bass cutting

The bass cut can also be executed with the same technique using the HPF – and may be even easier and more effective if the HPF is quite a harsh one. In fact, if the HPF is a particularly good one on your mixer, you may be able to mix together two tunes that you would otherwise never be able to overlap. If you are lucky enough

Careful and sophisticated use of EQ is fundamental when making a record.

to have both a dedicated HPF and a dedicated LPF on each channel, then you can even try the very advanced trick of combining a bass-heavy rhythmic groove with a high-pitched vocal, piano and/or percussive tune by engaging the HPF (or cutting the treble) on the channel of the former and engaging the LPF (or cutting the bass) on the channel of the latter at the same time. It takes a keen ear to hear tunes that might be suitable for this tricky combining manoeuvre – and it takes plenty of practice before you learn how to smoothly do the EQ or HPF/LPF moves at the right time and on the right beat so that it doesn't sound too jarring – but, when perfected, this can be a showstopper.

Random EQ effects

Another handy weapon in the DJ's arsenal (when you get a bit bored) is to use the HPF/LPF or EQ in an almost random fashion to create an effect rather like an Acid House record. Put a long tune on and hold the HPF knob in one hand and the LPF in the other. When a suitably repetitive and quite musically full section begins (you'll need to experiment to find one), slowly begin to turn the LPF and keep turning until you hit the maximum and the tune sounds horribly muffled. Immediately begin to slowly turn it back the other way and, when it has returned to the original position, begin slowly turning the HPF until you hit the maximum and the tune sounds very tinny, like a clock radio in the bedroom. As soon as you hit the maximum, slowly turn the HPF back to its original position. The overall effect should be quite psychedelic and disconcerting – but, so long as the beat is never lost, this can be a massive moment in any set. If you have no HPF/LPF controls on the channels, almost exactly the same effect can be performed using the bass and treble EQ knobs, provided they are powerful enough. If they are not, try using the bass EQ first and then the treble and mid EQ knobs at the same time for the other side of the move. If you have a control for setting the frequency of the bass EQ, use a setting near 100 Hz as the starting point for this move.

Lastly, it is handy to know that EQ can be used to cheat while you learn to beat mix properly. A little tweak of the bass EQ on the record being mixed out, to cut away a bit of the bass and bass drum, usually makes the DJ sound slightly better when beat mixing.

did you know?

A very simple but effective trick is to insert a 'fill' from record 2 (usually the last bar of a phrase in which the drums play a roll of a funky fill – such as the classic fill from Roy Ayers' *Running Away*) into the mix while record 1 is playing. The records must be running at the same tempo, though. As you will only use one bar of record 2 over record 1, there is room to be a bit looser with the matching and mixing.

Hot and three-deck mixing

'Hot mixing' is really nothing more than mixing in beats from a drum machine or sampler over the top of your mix. Provided you are able to match the tempo of the record to the running drum machine (which is obviously much easier using a computer DJ set-up), the method is pretty much the same as for mixing in another tune.

Three-deck mixing

This is champion stuff but, if you are feeling quite confident with your beat mixing skills, a third deck (plugged through a third channel on the mixer) can add a mental sixth-dimension to your set. Try beat-matching all three tunes and switching between them as musically and with as much groove as possible. The tricks described in the next chapter can also be mixed and matched and cut between to great effect. The combination of an interesting beat mix on the first two decks with an a cappella mixed over the top from the third deck is always an exciting part of a set when performed well with an interesting combination of tunes.

Lisa Lashes is a champion DJ who is renowned for the great atmosphere at her gigs.

Here four-times Irish DMC champion DJ Tu-Ki uses a sampler to enhance a three-deck mix with the help of DJ Savwar.

Adding effects

The third deck can also be used for adding in scratching, sound effects, or leaving an a cappella cued up to create a big breakdown before mixing in beats from the other two decks.

As an added bonus, if your third deck is a PDX-d3, you could keep it running backwards with a groovy rhythm playing and occasionally mix in backwards beats as fills or to add a big moment.

For the less ambitious DJs (as most of us are), just use the third deck for sound effects by keeping a sound effects record on it and mixing a bit of it in to give your mixes a bit of interest. This is also very useful for covering the sound when mixing between two records that don't drop or beat mix together very well, such as when you want to slow down the tempo, or introduce a new vibe.

want to know more?

- Equalization is explained in detail at http://www.harmony-central.com/Effects/Articles/Equalization
- And also at: http://www.music.columbia.edu/cmc/courses/g6630/Equalization.html
- Visit: http://www.bangingtunes.com for all things DJ

6 The advanced digital DJ

So, you might ask, why would anyone want to mix with CDs? You can't put your hand on a spinning CD and you can't see the grooves to know where you are. And, worse still, you're unlikely to find half as many classic tunes on CD as on vinyl. Yes, there are disadvantages, but there are also plenty of features which mean CD DJing is brimming with possibilities.

Digital quality and convenience

Here is where it might get a bit hairy. Some of you, having seen the word 'digital', may be tempted not to read on. You might be thinking this chapter is meant to make a convert of you. And you would not be far wrong – but fear not. As some famous music writer once sort-of said: 'I have seen the future of DJing – and it's analogue but also sort-of digital'.

Are CDs really that good?

Its not an 'either/or' situation. You can have your quality cake and eat the convenience as well. And, anyway, neither factor is what it seems at first glance. In some respects, the 'quality' of a CD is far better than that of either a vinyl record or a Digital Audio File (ignoring the fact, for the moment, that a CD is a kind of Digital Audio File). The noise level on a CD is incredibly low, the high frequencies are amazingly clear and crisp, and even after the 500th play a CD will sound better than the 50th play of its vinyl cousin. Vinyl junkies, however, will never stop pleading that there is

You can integrate MP3s and other audio files into your set as they offer an effective way to manipulate the sound in the same way as with vinyl records.

CD turntables are becoming more popular, as they create a convenient way to mix music discs seamlessly into your set.

some indescribable sound that makes vinyl 'unrivalled' and, in any event, most people agree that the bass response on vinyl is generally better and fatter.

Are CDs really that 'convenient'?

As for convenience – no contest. Basic operation of a DJ CD player is mostly self-explanatory. On most models, the tune is easily controlled with a massive 'jog wheel' on the deck's top which is spun to find the cuepoint. Pressing the 'cue' button marks a cue point that can be returned to instantly with a second press of the same button. Pitch can usually be adjusted with a familiar pitch control slider (or digital version) and some players offer a mega-useful 'master tempo' feature that allows you to change the speed without changing the pitch (i.e. the key of the music), which is obviously handy for big changes in speed without suffering the Mickey Mouse or Lazy Drunk problems alluded to earlier on page 84.

> **must know**
>
> The smallest (and most easily stored) digital audio file will be the MP3 version of the tune – though this will also be of the worst quality. If you really care about quality and wish to be an 'audiophile' DJ, use the formats '.wav' or '.aiff' which are the best quality, though they can easily take up more than 80 Mb per tune in your computer's memory.

CD mixing

Most DJ CD models offer two methods for cueing up: automatic and manual (though never in the 'with your hands on the music' kind of way). Here we teach you how to do both.

watch out!

Cueing up MP3 tracks is quick and easy, as you can save as many cue points as you like and keep them forever. But remember that cue points which work for one mix may not work for another and it may be necessary to store different cue points on the same tune for different mixes – and label them carefully so you don't get confused.

Two different methods

In the automatic mode, the player will find a desired song and stop, all by itself, a split-second before the first sound of the track. This method works quite well for drop mixing, but is less ideal for beat mixing, where you need to be in full control of the run-up to the first beat of the tune. Cueing up a CD manually is much more like traditional DJing, because it allows you physically to find the exact chosen spot on the CD using either a 'jog wheel' (a big rotary control) or a backwards/forwards button.

As usual, when cueing up the first beat of a phrase, the DJ must be able to recognize what the 'attack' of a drum note sounds like but, because the CD player tends to approach it so slowly, at first only the very beginning of the note (the 'attack') can be heard before scrolling on to the rest of the sound. It takes some getting used to, but most DJs soon start to recognize the attack of many different sounds and become adept at cueing just before it. Once you find the exact cue point, most models of CD player offer storage buttons to store and return to up to four or more different cue points.

Perfect timing

Once you get the CD cued, you'll then need to hit the play button at exactly the right time to throw the CD into play in time with the record that you're beat

Using the CD player's jog wheel feature, it is possible to manually wind a track forwards and backwards when cueing up.

mixing against. Again, this can take a little practice to learn just how quickly each model reacts and, therefore, exactly when to hit the button. With both tunes rolling, beat matching is done in the traditional way by adjusting the pitch control and then, using the pause and play buttons – or the forwards and backwards buttons – correcting the position until the tunes are running in synch.

Looping

As a natural extension of storing cue points, DJ CD players almost all boast a (vinyl-beating) 'Loop' function. Looping is the continuous repetition of a chosen section of a tune so quickly and smoothly that you could easily think the tune repeats that section on the CD itself. If the CD player has buttons marked 'loop in' and 'loop out', then you only need set loop points by hitting these on the fly (at the right time, as the CD is playing). Then, hit 'loop' at any

The Loop function on some CD players allows you to create looped portions of a track without departing from the mix.

point while the CD is playing in the middle of the loop. When the CD reaches the point stored in 'loop out', it will automatically and immediately return to the 'loop in' point and play on until the 'loop out' point. It will do this over and over – until you hit it again to let it play on. Conveniently, it always does this in the groove, without ever missing a beat.

If your player doesn't have a 'Loop' function, you can still do the trick using the stored cue points. Start by hitting the 'store cue' button for cue point #1 at the point you wish to begin the loop (usually the first beat of an 8-bar phrase). Then, after the CD has played through the phrase, hit the cue #1 button – the one that returns the CD to cue point #1 – just slightly before the first beat of the next phrase. The CD should play from the beginning of the previous phrase at exactly the moment when it would have played the next phrase. It should sound as if it was meant to repeat the section. With this method, you need to repeat the process for each loop you want each time (whereas the automatic method does it for you over and over).

With these functionalities for cueing, pitching and adjustment, drop mixing and beat mixing are performed in the traditional way with any 'hands on' adjustments being made via the 'jog wheel'.

It is possible to deliver an interesting and engaging set made up entirely from tracks on CDs.

The computer DJ and MP3 mixing

Two of the best things about MP3 mixing are having no record boxes to hump around and the easy availability of 'cheap' (that is, often free) digital audio files on the internet. Clearly, these features are hard to beat, especially when you are starting out.

Getting started

If you have never used a computer mixing program, start now by downloading one of the main cheap (or free) DJ mixing software packages and messing about with it (such as http://otsdj.com/ or http://www.mixvibes.com/mv4proeng.htm). Most offer nifty features like a 'BPM calculator', automatic cue storage and looping functions, and even automatic faders that do smooth fade ins and outs for you.

The computer DJ has two choices when mixing digital audio files: either download (i.e. purchase) one of the many all-in-one DJ mixing software packages and do the whole thing on-screen, or use some software-based element alongside your normal mixer and decks set-up. The first option is heavily dependent on the chosen product, as most of the computer DJ products are quite unique. Of course, each one has its own version of on-screen decks and a 'virtual mixer', but the mixing methods are all different and most have the disadvantage of having to mix with a mouse or a keypad. One alternative would be to use an on-screen package only as a 'player' (alongside other decks or players) and plug the audio output of your computer into the line input of a channel of your mixer. With this method, you could think of the computer just as a 'virtual deck' that happens to play MP3s and have the best of both worlds.

> **try this**
>
> One key advantage of PC DJing is that the computer will have a search function for your tunes library which can help inspire your set list. Searching the artist field, title field or genre field can throw up combinations and connections of tunes that might otherwise be difficult to spot.

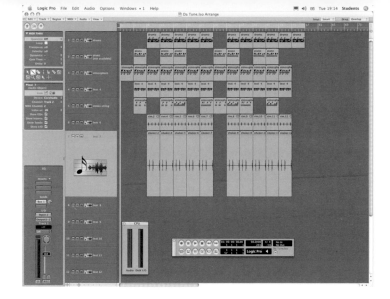

Computer software such as Logic gives the user an effective studio package for creating audio mixes.

Computer sound cards

Nearly all computers (PC and Macintosh) come with a built-in soundcard. Some have better quality audio than others and some have bigger or smaller leads that will need expensive adaptors for connection to a standard mixer. For most small computer set-ups, you'll probably need to use the computer's headphone socket to connect to your mixer but, ideally, you should have two separate outputs (one for the main output and one for the monitor output). But not to worry if you don't, as many people use only the main out anyway.

To cue the first beat of a digital audio file for beat mixing, simply press play until you hear the first sound and then press 'cue'. Next, move the track backwards in slow motion (rewind does this) until you find the top of the sound and then hit 'cue' again. The tune is now cued and ready to play. Load up another tune, cue it the same way and, if possible, enable the 'beat match' system (it will suss the tempos and do the necessary pitch control). Of course, as with the CD DJ 'master speed', the pitch and speed are independently controlled.

The computer DJ and MP3 mixing | 115

Ripping, burning, encoding and sampling

The digital CD DJ does face a problem in collecting tunes, because very few shops sell large catalogues of old, new and classic tunes on CD. The digital DJ, therefore, has to rely on wits. And computer expertise to 'rip' and 'burn' tunes.

Transferring digital music files

'Ripping' describes the act of loading music from a pre-recorded CD (which you already own, or perhaps have borrowed), or from some other source, onto your computer's hard drive. 'Burning' and 'encoding' describe the reverse procedure of transferring music files from your computer's hard drive onto a blank CD, though 'encoding' often refers to the level of quality you use for storing the file. If you are simply downloading files and mixing them from the computer or burning them onto a CD, however, then you generally need not worry about quality levels (as they will almost always be set at one of the standard MP3 encoding rates). However, if you are a confirmed audiophile, you should ensure that your chosen computer music program is set to its highest rate of quality (usually '320').

Sampling

'Sampling' is a confusing term, as it sometimes applies to a method for making records, sometimes refers to working with digital DJ programs and, most commonly, to using a CD player in a traditional DJ set-up to play a CD with special loops, sounds and sound effects on it. These snippets of sounds or loops can be dropped over an instrumental or spun-in from time to time to add excitement, much as some DJs use a third deck. The use of sampling from a CD is especially useful, however, because of the looping function which allows you to loop any of the snippets (and leave them playing in that loop all night) for use at any time on a split second's notice.

Some CD burners will take compact contemporary media such as the memory card shown, enabling a super-quick and easy download of digital files.

FinalScratch and Ableton live

Clearly the biggest problem for computer DJs is that, visually, it looks a lot of the time like they are just catching up on their emails and the audience may think that the whole show is pre-recorded. There are, however, ways of overcoming this problem.

FinalScratch

Mouse manipulation, aside from being not as fun as rotary wheel work, tends to make for a boring show. So thank God, then, for the amazing invention called 'FinalScratch', which allows the computer DJ to use an actual proper real turntable – instead of a mouse or keyboard – to control the computer.

This ingenious system works by using a special vinyl record (which you have to buy and it's the only record you use for the whole set). Instead of music, this record holds a constant stream of data (called 'SMPTE Time Code'); you don't listen to this data stream (it sounds horrible), but rather it

FinalScratch allows the perfect integration of vinyl technique and digital flexibility.

is played on a normal turntable that is plugged directly into the computer. The data that comes off the vinyl is read by the computer and is used to tell the computer where the digital audio file is to play. If you play the vinyl from the beginning, the computer plays the file from the beginning and, if you stop and rewind the vinyl, the computer does the same and the file sounds just as if you were playing it from vinyl. Spin it slow and it plays slow; Baby Scratch and it goes 'wukka wukka'. Beat matching, and everything else, works in the traditional way. It is so brilliant and works so well that it has to be seen to be believed.

Ableton Live

An interesting alternative to basic computer DJ programs is the product 'Ableton Live' which combines the conventional basics of computer DJ programs with a remarkably adept music production program that, amazingly, all works together in real time without missing a beat. Combining features that allow the DJ full hands-on expressive control with a robust and stable platform – reliable enough for live performance under pressure – 'Live' is both a DJ mixing system and a standalone musical instrument at the same time.

'Live' offers the DJ the ability to 'drop' digital audio files into the on-screen mix page, as well as add samples and loops and even offers MIDI compatibility for DJs who prefer a true musician-based approach. This revolutionary program is a quantum leap for DJs who wish to experiment with combinations of DJ skills, musicianship and live performance.

want to know more?

- See the homepage of Final Scratch at http://www.stantondj .com/v2/fs/index.asp
- Go to: www.pointblanklondon .com for information on digital DJing.
- Visit: http://www.mp3mach ine.com/win/MIXING_ DJ to try out computer DJ programs.
- Visit: http://www.mymusic tools.com/download/ dj for plenty of cool things to play with.
- The premier PC program for DJs can be found at http://www.pcdj.com
- If Ableton Live sounds like your world, check out www.ableton.com for more information.

7 Effects, tricks and scratching

Tricks are an essential addition to the DJ's set because they add life and soul and allow the DJ extra scope to make the mix their own. Never let it get out of hand or allow it to turn into an Olympic event but, equally, don't let too much time go by without inserting some kind of excitement to remind the crowd who is in charge. Make sure these added bits are spontaneous and have some relevance to the moment – no one wants gratuitous DJ tricks – but then no one wants a pre-recorded DJ, either. Keep it real. And keep it well-performed by practising hard at home.

Conventional FX (reverb, echo, delay, chorus)

Unfortunately, the 'conventional FX' listed below require that you have special gear but, if you haven't got any flash 'effects boxes', not to worry, as most DJs use only those tricks that can be performed with the standard DJ gear and two bare hands.

must know

For a big and exciting effect, try sending the sound of one record into a reverb FX box for just one beat and letting the resulting output of the box (the 'effect') ring out over your mix. The bigger and longer the reverb, the bigger the effect will be.

What are 'conventional effects' (FX)?

The word 'effects' (FX), to recording artists and musicians, usually refers to one of the conventional and traditional mechanical or electronic sound effects that appear on every record made since 1950: reverb, echo, delay, chorus or variations on these themes. DJs will often use these effects in their sets – if they are available on a mixer or from a dedicated box sitting next to the mixer and hooked up to it – but, unlike pop stars, they will rarely be subtle about it. Subtlety in this context would have no point; these effects are already on all records and, therefore, a little extra would in most cases be pointless and probably go unnoticed.

With these effects the key thing to remember is that each one has an 'in' and an 'out'. The idea is to 'send' the sound of the tune into the effect (usually only for a very short moment – probably not more than a single beat) and then mix the 'out' (the 'effected' sound coming out of the box) back into your mix by bringing it up a channel of the mixer. Every effects box and every built-in effects unit is slightly different (and sometimes very different) so you will, unfortunately, do well to consult the manual in every case for this topic.

Reverb

The first and most common of all conventional effects is reverb, which is simply an electronic replication of the sound of a room or some huge place. A very 'large' or 'long' reverb is meant to sound like Wembley or Carnegie Hall, while a very 'small' or 'short' reverb is meant to sound like a plain old room in your house. Used with great care, reverb gives a record a special and unified quality and adds a bit of class – clearly useless then for, say, a Techno DJ. Used very occasionally in short bursts of massive or especially quirky settings, a splash of reverb on a beat in the mix can shake up a set and wake up a crowd. Experimentation with each of the available settings is the only answer, though it is usually most effective to 'send' only one short beat or one short burst of a tune to the reverb unit and let the resulting 'spray' or 'ring' splash out over the mix and slowly die away on its own.

Echo and delay

The words 'echo' and 'delay' are often confused, as they are created by the same box but are used differently. An 'echo', as the name implies, is a single distinct repeat of a certain sound – like the common echo you hear when you yell across a valley ('Hello ... ... hello'). This is created electronically by a 'delay box' which, when a sound is 'sent' into it, simply records that sound and plays it back slightly later (or 'delays it') according to the 'delay time' which you set. This will mostly be between a few milliseconds – i.e. thousandths of a second – and about three seconds. By setting a very specific delay time, the sound can be made to repeat in time with the music. This is most

did you know?
The secret to mixing a great a cappella is to find a well-known vocal and mix it over a much-loved instrumental tune. The more surprising or shocking the combination, the better it will be – just so long as it works and sounds groovy.

watch out!

When editing a preset delay effect in a conventional FX box, don't change the preset delay times (as these will probably be forming the effect) but rather try changing the feedback, modulation and other parameters to hear subtle (and not-so-subtle) differences.

easily demonstrated by a tune which has a tempo of 120 BPM. You will remember from the earlier chapter that 120 BPM means that 120 beats occur in one minute and this means that one beat occurs every half-second (also known as 500 milliseconds). Therefore, if you set the delay time at 500 ms and send the tune to the box, the beats will be repeated exactly one beat later and create the sound of the tune playing in time with itself but one beat late. By the same token, settings of one second (a.k.a. 1000 ms), one and a half seconds (1500 ms), two seconds (2000 ms), and so on will probably sound very groovy and be useful as an effect in your mix of this tune. As with reverb, experimentation is the way forward, and it is quite effective to 'send' only short bursts of a tune to the reverb unit and mix the resulting repeated or 'delayed' sounds over the mix. Try using a bit of 'feedback' (which means repeats of the delayed sound and should not be confused with the horrid whine that hurts peoples' ears when the system isn't working properly), and let the 'feedback' of the delay slowly die away over the tune.

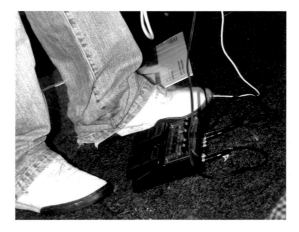

To keep your hands free for working the decks, a pedal can be used to trigger such effects as delay and reverb.

The Pioneer efx1000 is a good example of an all-round digital effects box.

Phasing, flanging and chorusing

When you use very short delay times on a delay box – less than 80 milliseconds – the repeated sound is too short to be heard as a distinct sound. With such short settings, the delay occurs at virtually the same time as the original sound but, if you mix together the original unaffected sound with the delayed sound, very interesting things happen. When the setting is between 1 and 10 ms, the mix of the 'before' and the 'after' creates the well-known psychedelic effect called 'phasing', which can be a very cool effect but which can make some people feel queasy if they hear it for too long. When the setting is between 10 and 30 ms, the effect is similar but less pronounced and is known as 'flanging', while any setting between about 30 and 80 ms is often described as sounding 'underwater' and is called 'chorusing'. All of these effects can be useful from time to time but, as you will expect by now, much experimentation is required. Also, don't forget that you need to 'send' the tune into the effect box and mix the output with the original tune in equal levels in order to hear the effect properly.

> **did you know?**
> Every sound you have ever heard – on record, in music, live on stage or in the bedroom – always has some kind of reverb on it. Sound with no reverb at all can only be heard in an 'anechoic chamber' (a specially-made 'dead' room) which scientists sometimes create for weird experiments on people's ears.

Switch and level tricks

The 'line/phono' switch located at the top of each channel on the mixer determines whether that channel will listen to its 'phono' input or its 'line' input on the back of the mixer. Used cleverly, this switch can create some awesome effects.

Quick switching

If you are DJing with vinyl, there would normally be nothing plugged into the line inputs (as the two decks are plugged into the two 'phono' inputs), so if you change the switch to 'line', you will hear nothing. In this scenario, the switch, when thrown, immediately and cleanly 'cuts' out the sound, which allows you to make rhythms with the tune plugged into that channel by toggling the line/phono switch quickly and rhythmically. This can be especially

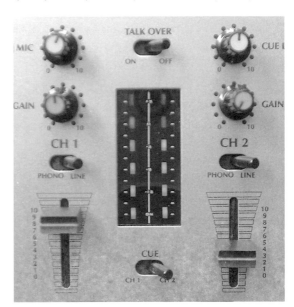

Changing the phono/line switch repeatedly and quickly in rhythm can create some interesting effects.

effective when used on a vocal or music section without drums, because it tends to create a sort of 'gated' or 'transformer' effect when you switch the sound on and off in rapid succession.

Another useful switch trick is to use the line/phono switch to 'isolate' just the booms of the bass drum hits. Flick the switch back and forth so that it is only in the 'phono' position when the bass drum notes play by turning it on only very briefly for each beat of the bar. Then, turn it off immediately after each bass drum hits so that there is a short silence between each bass drum. This trick takes a quick hand, and you may find it easier to use your finger or thumb as a 'spring' to tap out the rhythm against the pressure of one finger holding the switch in the off position.

If your switches are not designed suitably for these quick moves (or are broken or too noisy to use), this trick can also be performed as a 'level trick' with the channel fader by throwing it up and back down again very quickly. This is very difficult to do, however, and will never be as quick as the switch method.

Strobe

This very difficult trick consists of slowing the tempo down by using your hand to pause the record on every beat count, delaying one record against the other and fading back and forth between the tunes. The two records can be the same or can be of two completely different beats. Begin by slowing the first record and then delay the second by some groovy number of beat counts and alternately pause and fade between the decks. This trick is especially useful to slow down the tempo of your mix.

Spinbacks and other tricks

The spinback is basically just a swift 'rewind' of a short blast of a tune, so that a beat or two or three is heard again as a quick reprise. The trick often works well on the last beat of a phrase as you come out of the mix.

Grab the grooves

Immediately after the last beat sounds (or penultimate beat to allow a bit more time), simply grab the grooves and spin the record sharply backwards and straightaway crossfade to the new tune on the first beat of the next phrase, hopefully without missing a beat and always staying in the groove.

Some tunes work better than others, of course, and you may find that the search for the perfect spinback tune is long and hard. When you find it, though, you will have found a friend for life.

Spinning the record sharply backwards makes the track sound as though it is in rewind.

With prolonged use, especially when performing tricks, slipmats can become worn and should be regularly replaced.

If you find that a vinyl record won't spinback easily, it may be because the middle hole is too tight. You could try to carefully enlarge the hole with a pair of scissors, but take care not to do too much damage. Worse still, if a record is warped at all a spinback will usually just throw the needle off.

Try this easier version of the spinback trick mentioned earlier: instead of spinning the record backwards, just turn the turntable power off and let the record quickly grind to a halt. Then, crossfade over the new tune on the beat where it would have hit anyway (so as to keep the overall groove going for the dancers).

Back-to-back mixing

Back-to-back mixing is usually performed using two copies of the same record, though a true master may use anything. Start by beat mixing both copies of the same record and then nudge one of them enough so that it falls exactly one half of a beat behind the other. You should be hearing the bass drums of one record playing in the spaces between the bass drums

Perfect cueing skills will help greatly when preparing for a back-to-back mix.

of the other, therefore creating eight bass drums in each bar (between the two records). This isn't easy and sometimes it takes quite a few attempts until you learn to nudge it just that perfect amount.

Keep the crossfader hard to one side while cueing up and nudging, and then let the two tunes play (one half beat apart). Next, throw the crossfader over swiftly between bass drums, in order to add an extra bass drum from the second tune into the mix in between two bass drums of the other tune. Practise until you can perform a full back and forth throw in the space of one beat. Always remember to return the crossfader back to the original side after adding a bass drum so as not to confuse the beat and, whatever you do, never lose the main 1-2-3-4 groove (or you will have failed as a DJ and might as well give up and exchange this book at the shop for *need to know? Gardening*).

Phasing

This trick also requires two copies of the same tune and is similar to the 'phasing' effect achieved by the conventional FX boxes described at the beginning of this chapter (but much better and far more personalized). Start by beat mixing the two copies at exactly the same point so that they mirror each other in every respect. Beat mix them as tightly as you can and then throw the crossfader into the middle so that you can hear both records in equal volume. You should already notice that the sound of the two together in the speakers has that psychedelic quality. Try ever-so-slightly nudging one of them just enough to throw it very slightly out of time and, hey presto, the effect gets more intense. By then correcting them again, the phasing effect becomes even more intense. If you should happen to get the two records absolutely perfectly beat-matched, the entire sound of both records will momentarily disappear – and you can congratulate yourself on having achieved a perfect phase.

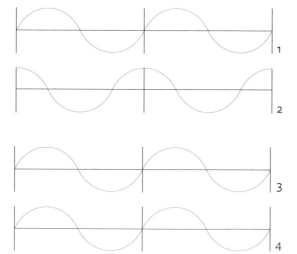

The first two waves are the same form but do not start at the same time, so they will clash and not phase. The third and fourth waves do start at the same time and therefore they will phase.

Fills

For this trick, you simply crossfade to the tune you are about to mix to as usual, but only for the last one or two bars of a phrase, and then return quickly back to the first tune, using the crossfader. The idea is to use the second tune only as a sort of 'drum fill' to introduce the next phrase of the original tune. Most DJs will do this at several points throughout the phrase (to 'tease' the crowd, who are expecting the new tune to drop). For extra credit, try creating new drum patterns in the first tune by switching back and forth between the two beat-mixed tunes quite often within a phrase or even within a single bar – which is like back-to-back mixing, but only for a short section and only as a set-up to a new section.

Beat-juggling

The key to beat-juggling (or 'making beats') is a great deal of patience and experimentation. Use your two copies of the same record again and cue them up with the crossfader in the middle. Play record 1 and, just as a drumbreak is about to end, start record 2 and straight away snap the crossfader all the way across to record 2. This is all about quick cuts between the decks – blending or beat matching is not required. You should be so certain of the positions of each record that, provided your push-off is spot on, there is no need to worry about beat matching. As the drumbreak on record 2 is just about to end, use the same process to get back onto record 1. Spinning the record back manually is the best way to get the break back to the starting point and, with practice,

try this

Creating your own CD filled with your favourite samples is a handy and very cost-effective way of making your live set more personal. Collect a load of records and CDs with useful loops and sound effects and spend a day editing them all together and burn it all onto one recordable CD (and label it carefully with correct timings).

Clever but sparing use of well-performed tricks adds excitement and originality to a mix, and the crowds love it.

you will learn how big a spin is required and will be able to spin it back almost without looking. So, in a nutshell, switch back and forth in this way to create a succession of breaks.

Once you get the hang of it, make the loop tighter by using only a two (or even one) bar break. Remember, the trick is about quick cuts and quick backspinning – keep it fast.

Scratching 1: from Baby to Chop

Scratching is a Rite of Passage for every DJ and, even if you plan on never performing a scratch in any set of your DJ life, it is worth learning just to improve your overall skills and dexterity. But first things first: make sure that your slipmat is very slippy indeed.

must know

If you do a lot of scratching, always carry a spare slipmat to use in case your normal slipmat should get wet from sweat, humidity or the odd beer spillage.

The Baby Scratch

The Baby Scratch is the most basic of scratches and forms the basis for all other scratches. For reasons that will soon be apparent, the Baby Scratch is also known as the 'wukka wukka'. The point here is simply to move the record back and forth under the needle in time with another tune. Improvization is a big part of it and you should jam any rhythm that moves you, so long as you stay funky.

Start with just one record on the first deck and cue it up to any big drum sound, but to make it easier stay somewhere near the outer edge. Using the same hand technique as you use for cueing and mixing, simply move the record sharply (or slowly) back and forth so that the one drumbeat (or whatever sound you've chosen) can be heard going forwards then backwards. The faster you pull and push the record, the shorter and higher-pitched the scratch will sound. Start getting some control over the sound by running another track on the other deck, and do a single scratch in time to it on the first beat and then on every beat of the bar. Remember to keep your hand well away from the tone arm and, if the needle jumps when you scratch, just try it slower until you develop better control.

Virtually any sound will work as a scratch, but it is probably best to start by trying to scratch various percussion and drum sounds. Until you gain proper confidence in your scratching, practise using varied sounds in time to a record with a quite slow tempo and gradually try faster tunes and more complicated rhythms.

The Forward Scratch

The Forward Scratch is a combination of a Baby Scratch with crossfader moves to 'chop up' or 'edit' the scratched sound. By using the fader at the right moment, you can lose part of a chosen scratched sound and keep the rest. For an easy example: a bass drum, when scratched slowly, will make a sound like 'cha – ka'. Using the Forward Scratch method, you might choose to lose the second part of the sound by throwing the fader over immediately after the first bit of the sound, thereby leaving only the sound of 'cha', without the 'ka' after it. This is usually done to the rhythm of a track playing on the first deck by keeping the crossfader over to the left and only throwing it to the middle for the short blast of the 'cha' sound from the Forward Scratch on the

Scratching requires thought, two-handed dexterity and plenty of practice.

must know

Scratching is a physical art that improves when the DJ is dancing. While performing scratches, try to move your body to the beat of record 2 (not the one you are scratching), so that the running tune controls the overall groove for the crowd.

second deck. The crossfader is then thrown all the way back to the left while you pull the scratch record back and set it up for another Forward. Keep thinking: open crossfader, forward pull, close crossfader, return record to original position. Keep repeating it as long you can and, as ever, make it sound rhythmic and funky.

The Backward Scratch

To perform a Backward Scratch, use the same crossfader technique, but reverse the scratch moves so that you start with the backwards move and return it again by moving forward.

The Scribble

The Scribble is a twist on the Baby. Do your Baby moves with a short break in between each scratch and then, by tensing your arm, shake your arm quickly but in a small movement so that it looks like your arm is freaking out. The sound should also sound like a bit of a freaked-out scratch as the music shimmers.

The Chop

You need some serious crossfader technique to do the Chop, because the moves are quick. Practise sliding it quickly back and forth by flicking it with your finger and thumb in time to the music, and remember that you need to do this without looking because you should always be watching the vinyl to remember the spot where you need to return to for the next scratch. The idea of the Chop is to chop (or 'edit') out part of a Forward Scratch so that only part of a sound is heard. The classic Chop is to use only the beginning or middle of a very recognizable word or sound so that the audience hears enough of the sound to know what record it is but is then teased over and over until finally you give them the Full Monty.

TIP: The Forward Scratch works particularly well when you scratch a word of vocal. Practise scratching the vocal word at an even speed so that the word is clearly heard and understandable when repeated over and over. Then practise closing the crossfader before pulling the vinyl back so that the audience doesn't hear it backwards when you're pulling it back.

TIP: Practise by recording yourself doing the Forward Scratch on a vocal word over another tune and listen for where the rhythm or scratching isn't even, or the word isn't understandable.

Coordination, timing and speed are all vital ingredients for making a scratch work with the track playing on the other deck.

Scratching 2: from Chirp to 'Tones'

Once you have got the hang of the more basic scratches, try moving on to these slightly more complicated scratch tricks.

The Chirp Scratch

The Chirp Scratch is about making bird sounds with your deck. For this scratch, you must be lightning fast enough to do the Forward Scratch and throw the crossfader at virtually the same time. Start with the record cued and the fader open and then push the record forward and close the crossfader at the same time so that virtually the entire sound is cut off – leaving only a small bit of sound at the beginning of the scratch. By allowing only the tiniest sliver of sound to be heard, the effect is like a bird call.

The Tear Scratch

A Tear Scratch involves making three separate sounds from one scratched note by quickly stopping and starting the record as you move it under the needle.

DJ QBert is considered to be the number one scratch DJ. He has invented many scratches as well as his own scratch unit.

Obviously, this requires some flash handiwork. The trick is to move the vinyl back and forth in a rhythmic way so that you play the very beginning of a sound, then pull it back about halfway through the sample, stop, and then pull it the rest of the way back. This 'forward–back–back' move can be repeated over and over and makes a useful change from normal-sounding scratches.

There are records produced solely for the purpose of scratching which contain various sound effects and loops.

The Crab Scratch

'Crabbing' also makes several sounds from one. This is not an easy trick, but it's impressive if you master it. Start by scratching a sound over and over in time to a tune on the other deck. Now put your thumb and fifth finger on the crossfader and click your fifth finger so that your fourth finger falls onto the crossfader. Now click your fourth finger so that the middle finger takes its place and finally click again so that the index finger joins the thumb on the crossfader. Of course, this will probably sound like 50 miles of bad road at first and it takes practice to get even the slightest resemblance to the real thing. The goal is to flick all the fingers so fast that the crossfader moves on and off fast enough to make an incredibly quick 'strobe' or 'gate' effect on the sound.

To get good at Crabbing, without using any records or sounds, practise by repeating the finger clicks to get comfortable with this weird move. Practise one click at a time in rhythm to a record at one click per beat. When it sounds even, move up to two and four clicks per beat. Ultimately, you should go so fast that, even though there is no groove, the four sounds are distinct and clear.

The Transform Scratch

The 'Transform' is the King of Scratches and always gets a reaction. The idea is to create a series of Chop scratches on a single sound so, when you practise, it's important to start by using a long sound (like a long vocal note on an a cappella mix). Push the record forward through the sound and, at the same time, use the crossfader to switch very quickly the sound on and off in the speakers as the tune plays. The result is like a 'strobe light' effect on the sound (or a 'gated' sound, if you prefer audio words).

The Hydroplane Scratch

The 'Hydroplane' is an interesting and uncommon scratch, done by gliding your finger(s) along the vinyl surface against the record rotation. The effect is a gritty and bassy sound which makes it seem like the music itself is vibrating.

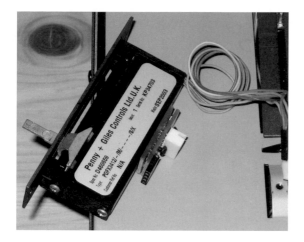

Crossfaders can wear out with constant use, and may need to be replaced from time to time.

The 'Tones' Scratch

'Tones' is also unusual and interesting to watch but requires that you buy a special record with only weird and eerie tones on it (usually it's a 'test tone' record used by broadcasters for the 'Emergency Broadcast System' – ask for it at a good DJ vinyl shop). The effect is to create a melody out of the tone by scratching the record and switching on short bursts of the tone noise while varying the pitch control to create different pitches. Not easy, but an amazing effect when done well.

TIP: Try the Chirp using first a drum note and then a vocal to see which sound creates the best effect for you.

TIP: The Transform is most effective if you turn the sound on and off in time to a record – very quickly – using eight or 16 'cuts' to a bar. Start with just one cut per beat and, when comfortable, move up to two per beat and so on. Most importantly (yet again and as always), keep it rhythmic and groovy.

want to know more?

- Visit your local music shop to try out Conventional FX boxes
- Tips for scratching can be found at:
  http://www.discjockey101.com
- Videos showing demonstrations of scratching are at:
  http://www.djkeltech.com/scratch.htm
- More tricks are described at:
  http://www.i-dj.co.uk/technique/techniquepage.php?ID=10

8 Getting and playing gigs

The range of earnings for a DJ stretches from zero to what might as well be infinity. A top international DJ might earn £30,000 for three hours' work while a hard-working-but-relatively-unknown DJ might earn £30 for a six-hour set (and have to hump all their own gear). To top it off, the jet-setter probably doubles their packet through sales of mix and compilation CDs, while their counterpart can barely afford to buy one. So how can an aspiring DJ get started on this road to fame and fortune?

Managers, lies and money

There is an uncomfortable tension between music and business, but you would never know this when you hear people talk about the Music Business. You do it for love, obviously, but records cost money and you always need more records... and more gear... and more records... and more gear...

The best way to get a gig

However good a DJ you become, you always face the problem of getting gigs. Unfortunately, it can often be about 'who you know' rather than 'what you know'. The biggest clubs and management companies can book the biggest gigs, but they are more likely to be impressed by a DJ who carries their own built-in audience. So it helps to have loads of mates (who, in turn, have loads of mates) that you can cajole into showing up when you need them.

Most DJs play gigs in clubs and bars, and the occasional event put on by a sound system company. Some clubs are well known – such as London's Fashion and Ministry of Sound – but most are not. Clubs make their money by charging an entrance fee on the door, selling food and drinks and also by money taken through gambling, video and other machines inside. In most cases, the door money gets divided between the promoter (who brings in the punters), the club (providing the premises) and the DJ (you). The club has to pay all the usual costs of running a business such as rent, bulk-buying alcohol and cigarettes and paying tax, and often the club will see the DJ simply as another expense. If the DJ is a normal jobbing DJ, they may take 20 or 30 per cent of the door

You might decide you need a
manager. Be careful, though –
there are some devious and
unscrupulous people working
in the music business.

takings but some successful DJs can earn three times
as much and more. If you play a club regularly and
pack it out every time, you should probably be setting
the door price yourself and taking all of it – and maybe
even a percentage of the booze takings as well, if
you're really popular and a good negotiator.

Who does what?

Many novice DJs assume that winning the interest
of a manager or a promoter is their ticket to fame,
fortune and big gigs, but most beginner DJs
probably don't even know the difference between
a manager and a promoter. Let's take a closer look
at the cast of characters:

If you are just starting out as a DJ, be wary of promoters who might try to fleece you for too big a commission.

- **What is a 'Promoter'?** – Clubs and events companies tend to hire promoters, who are supposed to be clever and imaginative organizers who know loads of 'the right people' to widely publicize clubs' nights and events. Even if they seem useless, any working promoter will probably be helpful to you in getting a gig or two. Promoters tend not to be too closely connected to any one DJ, but a working relationship for some period of time may be enough to launch a regular circuit to keep for many years. A promoter may work for a commission of about 10–20 per cent of a tour, a fixed fee, or may be paid by the venue or event company.

- **What is a 'Manager'?** – A manager is simply anyone that claims to manage an artist and/or a DJ. In reality, however, and to be of any use to you, they need to have good contacts, good business and public relations (PR) sense – which many don't have, so beware. A manager will normally work for a commission of 15–20 per cent of the gross of all your fees.

- **What is a 'Club Manager'?** – Having a club manager (the guy who runs the venue night after night) for a friend is great for getting on the guest list and the occasional free drink, but to get regular gigs you'll need the club manager to introduce you directly to the managers and promoters that he or she knows. Remember, however, never to offend a club manager as, even if they can't personally get you a gig, they do have the power to make sure someone doesn't get a gig at their club.

- **What is an 'A&R Man'?** – A friendly 'A&R' (Artists & Repertoire) man (or a 'Record Company executive') is usually quite useful for getting free or un-released records, but they have no say in booking DJs. On the other hand, if you're looking for a record deal, you should probably seriously consider hanging out with him constantly and doing absolutely anything he asks....

- **What is a 'PR'?** – Public relations people help promoters and club managers and owners to publicize club nights, events, tours and acts. They probably can't help a DJ get gigs (though they probably know a man who can) and, as they often know everyone who is anyone, be careful what you say.

- **Can I get any help from 'Doormen' and 'Bouncers'?** No, but you can probably get a date or a drink. Whatever you do, though, don't get on the wrong side of these guys, as they can help get you into the club more quickly and on nights when you're not working.

Most DJs, at the beginning of their career, try to get gigs by applying straight to the owner or promoter of a club – but no doubt you'll soon be thinking of trying to find a manager (or management agency) to represent you. A manager has to spend a lot of time doing boring organizational stuff and usually has to take the blame for whatever goes wrong (rightly or wrongly). If you decide to look for a manager, try to find somebody who seems to know a lot of people in the business very well, is worthy of your trust (as far as you can tell) and, crucially, doesn't have too many other DJs on their books already.

It is always a good idea to keep on the right side of night club bouncers...

Finding your own gigs

Finding a manager is usually near-impossible for a DJ just starting out, so try using phone books, websites, local guides and newspapers to make a list of all the managers and agencies (and promoters) you can find.

Exploring possibilities

When you first make contact with managers and agencies, remember to note what other acts they claim to have on their roster and ask about their success in finding them gigs. If you can't find out from those sources, try ringing them up (stay anonymous at first and just say you're an interested DJ) and ask them who they 'handle'. This exercise should give you an idea about the possibilities that are out there for you (and, if nothing else, about the other DJs competing against you locally).

In a local context, a 'sound system' company is like a mobile club for rent (known also as a 'mobile disco'). The DJ(s) and their gear get hired out (complete with lights, decorations and catering) for events, corporate 'hospitality' functions and private parties. For younger DJs who can't work in bars and clubs, this can be a useful way to get gigs – and a serious learning experience, as you'll have to carry all the gear, set it up, take it down and hump it away. You might think of it also as a way of getting fit.

As the saying goes: 'What happens if you don't advertize? Nothing.' So, to get gigs, you have to let as many people as possible know that you exist. Here are a few ways to shout about yourself:

Creating your own website can be an efficient and effective way of publicizing yourself as a DJ.

- **Make a load of Demo Mix CDs** and give them out generously – and make sure your name and numbers are clearly displayed on both the packaging and discs themselves.

- **Print business cards**, carry them around at all times and give them out generously. They're relatively cheap to make – just make sure that your name and correct numbers are clearly displayed.

- **Approach the local newspapers**, as many are keen to report on local young musicians and DJs.

- **Create your own website** (or get a page on someone else's website). It can't hurt and your potential clients probably use the web for finding local talent, checking backgrounds and references.

- **Get into 'free listings'** in local newspapers, magazines, council and church bulletins and publications. Most will feature a 'listings' page or 'bulletin board' and they're almost always free. Make sure your current gigs are, if at all possible, listed in there – and see if there is any scope for providing a 'bio' – a short summary of your career as a DJ.

Making a demo mix CD

Aside from publicity, making a demo CD is the best way of improving your skills because it makes you suffer through your own mistakes and bad record choices and enjoy the good bits and top tune choices. All you have to do is record yourself mixing. Ideally, you would want to record your best-ever set but, a more realistic goal is to capture a decent set of which you can be reasonably proud.

Recording a set

In recording a set, you have two choices – do it at home or at a gig. Some people tend to 'rise to the occasion' at a gig or may need the pressure and excitement of a crowd to perform well so they will clearly prefer to record a real gig. Most of us, however, prefer being alone in a quiet bedroom with a cup of tea, where we can make mistakes and start over without embarrassment. If you do decide to record a live gig – say, at a friend's party – you need

Ideally you should 'burn' your own demo CD using a software like Toast.

only find some machine capable of recording sound, connect the master outputs of your mixer to the inputs of the recording machine and get mixing. The quality of the recording is one of the least important factors – even a cassette machine will do, if that's your only option – because nobody will be buying it for audio quality. In any case, the loud volume of most dance music means most noise from the tape will not usually be heard. Of course it would be better to use some kind of recordable CD machine – or even a computer capable of recording digitally – but don't sweat it.

If you have access to proper recording facilities then so much the better, but don't worry if your first demo is made on an old cassette recorder in your bedroom.

The best method

The usual method is to record your mix at home with a borrowed or rented machine, such as a:

- **Cassette machine** – if you do use a cassette tape recorder, try to borrow one that has two speeds and then use the better-quality fast speed.

- **Reel-to-reel** – always better than a cassette machine but hard to find, way-finicky and generally more hassle.

- **Recordable CD** – a good option (if you can find one) because it's the easiest to copy – though you might waste a few CDRs trying to get a good take, so buy in bulk.

- **Computer** – if you have access to a digital recording software set-up on a PC or Macintosh, then this is the best possible option. Not only is the quality quite good, but you have the possibility of recording many different takes of your set and then, afterwards, going back and editing the best bits together to create one 'perfect' set. This may seem like cheating, but, hey, grow up already. Even Elvis was edited.

Whatever option you choose, the connections will always be the same: master output of the mixer to the record input of the recording machine. When recording at home, monitor the sound if at all possible as it comes out of the recording machine rather than from the usual output of the mixer, because this will ensure that you hear exactly what is being recorded. This way, you or a friend can also check to see that everything's being recorded properly. When you finish a take, listen back carefully and note the good and bad points and, obviously, change the next take accordingly.

When making your demo CD, always, always, always:

- **Choose good tunes** – the most important thing you can do is choose top records for the set. Most of your audience will probably not be DJs, so they'll never notice the technical skills or mistakes – they'll just notice the music. The music you choose needs to fit with your intended audience and it also needs to be true to your own musical taste. Keep it real.

- **Mix loads of tunes** – remember that this is a short demo CD, not a night out. You need to show that you have lots of excellent records and that you know how to chop and change them competently and with style.

- **Don't worry about small mistakes** – remember you're not playing to a TV audience of millions. Your choice of music is almost everything.

- **Show off a bit** – of course you need to choose the best tunes and mix them smoothly, but you also need to prove that you are the most happening DJ in town. Throw in a couple of your best tricks, so long as they don't come too fast.

Top demos and DJ mix tapes will usually have been painstakingly edited to combine all the best takes – don't be too precious about the 'live' or 'all in one take' thing.

'The better the gear, the better the quality', but it won't matter unless the music is kickin'.

- **Keep it short and sweet** – one hour is about as much as most people will ever listen to.

- **Use the best gear you can** for the recording and clean your records first. If possible, get help from an experienced DJ who will sit with you for an afternoon to help ensure it all goes well.

- **Keep a constant volume** – the listener doesn't want to have to adjust the volume while listening.

- **Have fun** – this is not your debut solo album, it's your demo CD. People want to hear good tunes mixed well with the odd cool trick – not a self-indulgent, free-form art experience.

- **Update regularly** – make a new demo CD at least once a year (if not more often) so that you don't sound stale. Experiment with new tricks when you update your demo, so that you can show people that your DJ skills are steadily progressing.

- **Copy it as cheaply as possible** – burn your own CDs at home if you can but don't make too many at first (you don't want a garage stacked full of out-of-date demo CDs).

Always keep in mind the 'Big Picture': how the mix will sound as a whole. Even if every tune is banging, a set with no overall shape will be lost on your audience. Plan a sensible beginning, middle and end. This could mean starting out mellow, rising to a frenzied peak and coming down again, it could mean playing full-out from beginning to end, or it could mean something totally new and revolutionary. Whatever you choose, keep it real.

And short. Most managers, promoters, club managers and owners are likely to be pressed for time and, consequently, your demo CD may only get played for the first ten minutes. If this happens, is the beginning exciting enough? Do you get through more than two tunes in ten minutes? Are there are any tricks or exciting bits?

Also consider what your demo CD looks like. Without being overly flash or plain stupid, use a label and cover design that stands out – and whatever you do, don't forget to write your name and contact numbers clearly on the CD itself and on any packaging. Good luck!

Knowing your client and choosing records

When you do finally get a few gigs, your first concern must be your tunes – have you got the records you need to successfully pull it off? Do you know who is going to be there and what sort of music they will like?

must know

A perfect set needs a few instant highs and lows, usually created by big drops and breakdowns, a cappella mixes, huge hits and recognizable tunes, new tunes with old samples and old classics with a good trick or two as well as the occasional 'stab' of a well-known fill or sample.

Doing your homework

Consider all the factors necessary to make a good guess as to who the audience will be: the venue, the time of day, the season, the occasion, the door price, and anything else that may affect who is likely to show up and what ages they are likely to be. If you haven't got the right records – and you can't afford to buy them and don't know anyone to borrow them from – you cannot realistically do the gig. If you are in any danger of hurting your reputation and/or your wallet (from having to pay back your fee for a disastrous flop during a gig you never should have accepted), then you must refuse the gig. If you do not face these dangers and really have nothing to lose, then you may as well decide to take the gig and make the best of it. After all, a gig is a gig and a quid is a quid.

Choosing records and preparing set lists

For your first few gigs it makes sense to plan as much and as far in advance as possible. Draw up a draft set list and practise it all the way through at home. Make sure you have enough variation in genre, tempo,

You can never have too many records or too much money to spend on new records.

energy and well-known/obscure records. Think about what tricks work best for which tunes and ensure that those tricks are as evenly spread as possible. If in doubt, try on a different order or chop and change to experiment. Spontaneity is important, though if your set is too wild you may risk losing the crowd and could scupper your chances of another gig. You need to find a comfortable balance.

On the other hand, as time goes by you must fight the natural tendency to go stale. If you play the same tunes for more than a month of gigs, this is a bad sign. Keep listening – always listen – to new tunes (at least five a day as a general rule for a working DJ) so that your sources are wide and fresh. A constantly changing and varied mix of the hottest new tunes, interesting and groovy current bubblers, classic oldies and rare gems makes a DJ healthy, wealthy and wise.

Setting up the gig

The best possible preparation for a gig at a new venue is to visit it beforehand at least once and hear someone else play. If you don't do this, you stand absolutely no chance of making the right choices for your own set.

Check it out

Check out the crowd, keeping in mind that the time of day, season and occasion may be different when you play it. Check out the sound system, and move around to hear it from each corner, out in the middle and at the bar. Bring a notebook for a few discreet memos to remind yourself about any bass trap in the corner, boomy dancefloor or weird stereo effects. There might be lots of other factors that concern you – it all depends on the individual venue. Just use all the knowledge and awareness that you have accumulated to date and don't take anything at all for granted.

Check out the DJ booth well in advance of your set and make sure that everything is working and properly set-up.

Talk to other DJs

If possible, talk to other DJs who have played the venue to learn about the people to stick to and those to avoid, any house rules that you should know about, drinks in the DJ booth, times to start and stop, requests you must honour and any problems that may arise regarding money. All in all, it's like a detective mystery that you must solve: ask loads of questions, listen carefully to what everyone says, observe people and places carefully and, whenever necessary, take notes. The more you know, the less likely you are to fail. Remember – knowledge is power and information is everything.

Get out onto the dancefloor and listen to your sounds in the same way that your punters will hear them.

Warming up the audience

The only thing worse than going on straight after a terrible DJ who has bored and offended the crowd is going on after a genius DJ who has brought the crowd to the peak of ecstasy and coolly back down again, leaving them nearly for dead with only memories of the best tunes they ever heard.

Sensible precautions

Whether you are following a good or a bad DJ, you'll have to win over what is in effect a hostile audience. To avoid this kind of unfortunate surprise, it is always best to treat every crowd as a hostile crowd that will take your very best pulling power to win over. In other words, expect the worst and you'll never be disappointed.

It is always important to arrive at the venue at least a few minutes before the start of your set (even if you know the venue very well), so as to check out the crowd and see how they are reacting to the DJ on just before you. One of the worst things that can happen to a DJ is to discover, too late, that their opening tune

The DJ's boss is the audience – always keep the boss happy at all costs.

was played by their predecessor as their penultimate record. There will always be an element of luck in this, but at least you can try to arrive early enough in each case to hear the last couple of preceding tunes and avoid the most glaring clash.

The warm up

The first few tunes of your set – the 'warm up' – must be tailored to the specific gig. If you arrive to find that the previous DJ has ended on a massive high, then you might decide to give them a rest by starting with the cooled-out intro tune that you had always planned for. Alternatively, if the last few tunes before you go on are all mellow, you might decide to start your set list further in, with some up-tempo and more energetic tunes to get the party started again. You'll need to check the vibe and try to fit in as best you can.

Reading the crowd

Once you're into the body of your set, you still need to constantly check out (or 'read') the crowd to stay with them. The best mixing in the world will be lost on a crowd that just isn't in the right mood. Keep tabs on movements to and from the middle of the dancefloor and keep checking the bar to see if the queues grow or thin out. If you're playing a brand new venue and have come with a mate, it might be helpful to enlist them as a spy to bring you regular updates on audience reaction. Do whatever you have to do in order to keep abreast with what's happening. Never stop reading the crowd and, if you think you might be losing them, think on your feet and adjust your tunes accordingly. This is the most important goal of any DJ in any venue anywhere in the world. If you lose your audience, you'll have lost a gig.

watch out!

The most common complaint about DJ's sets is that they are just 'performing to themselves' and not playing to – and for – the crowd. If your audience isn't dancing, then you aren't succeeding, so keep your eye on the dancefloor. Never let your dedication to a particular style overtake the needs of the audience. After all, whoever pays the piper calls the tune.

Choosing the next record

Assuming you've got the crowd with you and you're reading them like a brilliant book, you've still got to keep questioning your set list: is the plan going to work? Even if you have drafted a genius set list with evenly-placed thrills and tricks, more often than not something will arise to throw you off it.

must know

Nobody can mix forever. Think about when to play long tunes which will allow you to have a quick break for natural (or unnatural) resuscitation. But always remember that everything takes longer than a DJ tends to estimate and all records are shorter than you think they are.

Is the plan working?

The volume and quality of the sound system may be such that the loudest part of your set is starting to grate, you may find that the DJ booth monitors aren't good enough quality for the difficult mixes and tricks in your plan and – this can easily become a nightmare – you may be faced with requests. All of these potential hurdles can force you to change your planned set list, so you must be prepared at all times to be flexible. React as sensibly and as coolly as possible and keep a couple of emergency crowd-pleasers at the back of your box to pull out and play if you need a few minutes to think. If you do change plan, try to keep the Big Picture in mind – don't get too focused on any certain tune or vibe at the expense of the set's overall pace. Try if possible to return to the set list, keep an eye on your watch and be aware of how many tunes you have left. Like the pilot of an aeroplane, you're in trouble if you over- or under-shoot your last move.

As for requests, a punter's request for a specific tune is less of a problem as it can usually be fobbed off with an earnest and regretful 'sorry, I haven't got it with me tonight', while a request for 'something faster' or (the worst) 'something slow' is harder to deal with – especially if it comes from the owner's wife or

React as calmly as you can to requests and think carefully about the bearing that they will have on the remainder of your set.

daughter. There's no easy answer for this problem (and you may need to simply comply as soon as practically possible), but one possible solution is to see if you can talk them out of it without them realizing. Try saying the names of a few records (like the ones you intend to play anyway) until you hit on one they react happily to – then say 'I love that too, and I'm about to play a tune just like it only better'. This approach occasionally works and, even if it doesn't at least you've managed to have a friendly conversation and not simply said 'no, now go away' (though in the end you may resort to something similar, out of pure desperation).

Closing the set

The last tune of the set may or may not be important depending on when you finish and who goes on after you. Some DJs have built a career on going on late and finishing with some ridiculous tune as 'last tune of the night' that everybody remembers and consequently loves them for forever. Some DJs are only ever remembered for the Big Tune in the middle of their set. It's always horses for courses. Don't get too hung up on it: the last tune is rarely as important as the twenty that preceded it.

Working with an MC

A DJ who uses a microphone is not a DJ – at least not in the sense that we have been learning about in this book. You may, however, one day find yourself plugging a microphone into your mixer in order to accommodate an MC.

Dealing with surprises

Clearly, like a pop band, you wouldn't ideally go out to play a gig without having worked out what you're each going to do, not to mention having rehearsed it endlessly. Unfortunately, however, all too often such 'spontaneous' performances are foisted upon a DJ at the last minute – usually by a rapper or MC marching up to you and saying 'here, plug this mic in and play some hip hop instrumental tune'. If you do ever involuntarily work with an MC, there's not much for it

If you work with an MC, try to remain in control and do not let him or her take over your set. Sometimes easier said than done.

Some DJs like to be their own MC – occasionally circumstances demand it – but this is the only time a DJ ever really needs a microphone.

but to listen and watch carefully and make sure the mic is never louder than the tune itself. If possible, the DJ can help most crucially by 'riding' the mic (turning it up and down as necessary) and adding a bit of EQ to help the crowd hear and understand the words. If you are particularly confident and good with effects, you might try adding a bit of reverb to the MC's voice to help them blend with the music. If in doubt, always err on the side of keeping the music louder than the mic.

The DJ's job is to keep the crowd dancing and, hopefully, the MC knows this. A good MC will know where to stand – facing the audience and playing to them but not directly in front of the DJ – and will put on a bit of a show without actually pulling the mic lead hard enough to rip it out of the back of the mixer. Most importantly, you can only hope that the MC knows when to shut up.

Practical arrangements and legal matters

Aside from getting the gig in the first place and going down a treat with the crowd, the most important thing is to get paid. Unfortunately, though you'd think this would be a formality, this crucial part of the job often goes wrong: either the DJ gets less than they thought they were owed or they get nothing at all.

Agreeing terms and conditions

The main thing to remember when you book a gig is that, whether the terms are written down or just agreed in a quick conversation, an 'agreement' has been reached and, if you can prove what was agreed, the agreement is legal. Hence, theoretically, if you have the money, the nerve and a good lawyer, it can be enforced.

The best way to improve your chances of getting paid is always to write down the terms of the agreement as soon as possible. Ideally, you would have a separate contract for each gig, dated and signed by the person (or someone representing the company) that will be paying your fee. If you can't get a written contract or cannot get them to sign it, the next best thing to do, as soon as possible after the verbal agreement and at least always on the same day, is to write out the terms that were agreed on a piece of paper and sign it yourself. It would also be helpful to have a witness. If the worst comes to the worst, at least you've got some evidence of the agreement – and that's always better than nothing.

Sort out all the practical arrangements of how and when you will be paid *before* the gig. Never let your hands be tied by unscrupulous operators.

When discussing the terms of your engagement as a DJ, always make sure that you agree at least the following: the fee and whether it includes VAT or not, the date(s), the exact start and stop time(s) of your set, what time you are expected to show up beforehand, whether you will have a sound check, exactly when (the day and time) you will be paid and how you will be paid (cheque or cash).

want to know more?
Take it to the next level
- See:
  http://www.thedjlist.com, a massive directory of DJs.
- Visit:
  http://www.djadvantage.com/index.php for loads of useful DJ stuff.
- The website http://www.trugroovez.com is a site of sites, providing links and references.

9 Making hit records at home

There is a very fine line between a DJ and a pop star and, the chances are, it won't be long before you start exploring the possibilities of jumping over it. It's inevitable really: nobody knows more about records than a DJ, so it's perfectly natural that the DJ should make records himself. Indeed, DJs have long proven that, presumably because they study records more closely than the rest of us, they are generally very good at producing them. Never mind that DJs usually know nothing about the music business and have never been in a recording studio – it's a DJ's God-given right to make records. And why not?

The home studio

Traditionally, the most costly aspect of setting up a studio was the designing and building of a space that kept the sounds you want to hear in and all others out. But, unless you intend to record a full band playing together live, you can avoid all of that expense. You only need a table, a chair, a computer, some old records and loads of patience.

The studio in your PC

It's only ten or fifteen years ago that anyone wanting to make a 'proper record' needed a recording studio that was worth a million to buy and cost a thousand per day to rent. It was an exclusive club, open only to those deemed worthy by the God-like record companies and rarely accessible to those 'non-musicians' called DJs. Occasionally, a DJ could visit a studio for a day to do a 're-mix' but generally that's where it stopped. Not any more.

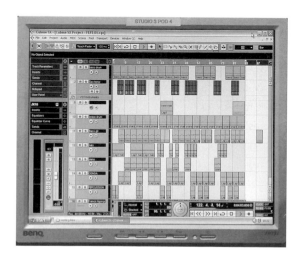

Nowadays nearly everyone can afford a PC and a basic music editing software such as Cubase.

There is something especially satisfying about having your own DJ set-up at home.

In case you were unaware of the fact, there is a recording studio in your PC and it's waiting for you to start using it. Unbelievably, this computer-based recording studio is virtually as good-quality as the million-dollar studio of late last century. And it's much easier to use. There are, as you would expect, dozens of music production software applications to choose from, ranging from very cheap and easy (such as 'GarageBand') to quite complex and expensive (such as 'ProTools'). The three most popular and best programs, at least for DJs, are: 'Logic', 'Cubase' and 'Ableton Live'. All three programs ideally should be used with a decent-quality 'soundcard' installed in your computer, which you probably already have, if you are using a Computer DJ program to mix. Each of these computer-based music production tools is used to make 'proper records' everyday in expensive studios (and in cheap bedrooms) in London, LA and everywhere in between.

The great advantage of these programs is that they cater to all kinds, including those using the 'MIDI' approach to recording with synthesizers and drum machines, those preferring the microphone-based 'digital audio' approach using digital recording to

If you become seriously successful as a DJ, who knows - maybe one day you could have a home studio as grandiose as this one!

record live players singing and playing instruments into mics, and the most user-friendly 'sample-based' approach in which bits lifted from other records are manipulated, re-organized, twisted, turned inside-out, overlapped and spun into groovy new records. This last style of recording is a favourite of DJ producers (such as Fatboy Slim and De La Soul) who are already well used to mixing and re-interpreting records and find that this approach to recording comes naturally to them.

While there are a million details to learn for each program if you insist on becoming a world-class expert, the basics are very simple, take only minutes to learn, and allow you to make records with top-quality audio remarkably quickly.

Building a collection of sounds

So where do you get your raw sounds to work with from? Well, one option is simply to use the sounds that come with the program straight out of the box. It's cheap, quick and simple. But it's also boring, because you would be using only the same sounds as every other kid on the block. A second, and more interesting, option is to buy one of the many 'Sample CDs' of sounds available in music shops and via ads in music magazines and the internet. These CDs come in every imaginable version: sound effects, drum loops, guitar riffs, piano licks, a cappella vocals and just about everything else. Again, the problem is that you are very likely soon to use some sound that someone else has also just bought and has also just loaded into their Cubase (or Logic or Live) computer production program. Alas, as in life, the only way to be truly original is to do it yourself – that is, sample your own sounds from your own records – and there is no reason why any DJ cannot do this themselves. All it takes is knowledge of records, a wire to connect the deck to the computer and the patience to edit the bits you record.

If you are intending to record vocals, ensure that you soundproof the room thoroughly first in order to keep out background sounds.

The home studio | 173

The recording process

Once you have collected a body of loops and other raw sounds to work with, the process is all about trial and error: what would it sound like if a booming four-on-the-floor kick drum was pasted under that one-bar funky drum loop? Or if a simple drum loop was combined with that guitar lick and this a cappella vocal?

must know

The process of recording one track at a time – usually starting with the kick drum, then adding a snare drum and high-hat, then a bass line and so on – is called 'overdubbing' and is the basis for all studio recording. The process of automatically correcting the timing of your musical performance, after you have recorded it, is called 'quantizing' and is easily done on computer-based recording systems and drum machines.

Deciding what to record

How about if the loop were repeated three times followed by the same bar put in backwards as a one-bar fill? If the whole thing had a bit of reverb and phasing? And what about a breakdown ending with a spinback leading to a repeat of the whole thing?

This is the stuff of modern recording and studio etiquette now means coming up with good ideas and being patient while the idea is executed. The process is without boundaries, other than the length of a day and the limit of human patience.

Recording with singers and instruments

The day may come when you find yourself bored with samples and loops and breaks and long for a real singer on your music – and there is no reason not to bring it on sooner. Recording with a microphone is possible and very simple with almost any computer music production program. The hardest part will probably be finding a decent mic. It really is as easy as putting the mic on a stand, connecting it to your computer's sound card and hitting the record button. Of course you would be wise to try to get the best sound possible

Instruments should be recorded separately from vocals, ideally in a sonically 'dead' room.

by setting up the mic in a sonically 'dead' room (such as a small room without parallel walls, or a hallway with a blanket hung on one side) and using one of the 'compressor' programs available on-line as an auxiliary program (an example of a 'plug in') so that the level of the singer is automatically controlled. And you'll probably want to use a bit of reverb to soften the voice and make it soar more freely in the mix. But, even without these 'plug in' extras, the addition of original recordings such as vocals, guitar, electric bass, whatever, will almost certainly and instantly lend more excitement and life to your music. As with all music (and as in life), experimentation leads to a richer and more interesting experience.

watch out!

Record live vocals in a quiet room with windows closed and blankets on the wall to avoid unwanted traffic noises, room echo and other unwanted sounds.

Record deals

Though there are fewer major record companies than in the old days, and 'big hits' tend not to sell as many copies, the record business is still healthy and deals are still out there waiting for you.

Getting your deal

Unfortunately, you have to travel farther to get to them now and the queues are longer for the few record executives and A & R ('Artists and Repertoire') people still around and waiting to hear your stuff. Also, the concept of a 'demo' has radically changed, because the companies expect you to present a top-quality finished mix for them to judge. If they like it, you may get an offer and, if you accept the offer, the record is quite likely to be released just as you mixed it. To be sure, there are still record deals which involve you moving to New York for three months to record your new album with some flash producer hired by the record company at great expense, but the majority of deals now go to artists who have recorded and mixed their tunes themselves – and an enormous number of those artists do so using a Cubase (or Logic or Live) computer music production program.

Releasing your own records

If you are unable to catch the attention of a record company (or cannot be bothered to join the very long queue of artists trying to get their tunes listened to), the other option is to release your music yourself on your own 'label'. In the bad old days, this meant putting up a ton of money to pay for the pressing of expensive CDs (or vinyl discs), having them transported to record shops, doing all you could to publicize your record and

This state-of-the-art Vestax vinyl disc cutter would be a handy thing to own as a home-based record maker.

hoping that people went to one of the right shops to buy a copy. Of course, this has all long since been changed by the advent of digital recording, home CD burning and online distribution.

Many DJs now make their own tunes and sell them as downloads via as many websites as they can get onto (ensuring that they are always in a 'non-exclusive' arrangement with each site or digital distributor). Most also burn their own CDs at home and sell them directly to punters in clubs from a table at the door or straight from the DJ booth. Some DJs will set up their own small company through which to run the business and the accounts for selling their music and most tend to put the name of that company on the label of the CD – and in this way they will have set up their own record label to distribute and sell music.

It really is as simple as that and it's going on all over the world and getting bigger every day. The process hasn't quite killed off the major record companies just yet (and if you sell enough copies of one of your records, it is likely that one of those majors will find you and buy you out for loads of money), but it's not hard to imagine a world very soon where such 'independent labels' are the norm.

Making mash-ups and using samples

The simplest way to make a record – and most DJs do this every time they mix – is to combine one record with another in a new and pleasing way and, hey presto, new tune. This is very likely to be the way most DJs begin their recording career.

Re-mix to new record

By simply doing the kind of mixing they do every night in clubs, but recording the combined sound onto a digital recorder or into a computer music production program for further editing and mixing, DJs create new records as a matter of course. Whether you call the resultant end product a 'new record', a 'mash-up', a 're-edit' or a 're-mix' is a matter of taste, but the result is the same and, if it's good, people will want to hear it. If it is very good, people will want to buy it. But is this legal – is a DJ allowed to do that?

Samples

To pay or not to pay? That is the Sample Question. If you use a sample from an old record, then legally the owner(s) of the copyright in that old music are entitled to some kind of compensation. So what's a poor boy or girl to do? Of course, you could do what they used to do in the Bad Old Days: sample first, ask questions later. However, this was a wildly dangerous approach, reflecting the Wild West-style standards by which dance music musicians lived in those days.

Back then, so much was different – the lawyers didn't understand the technology, the law in general

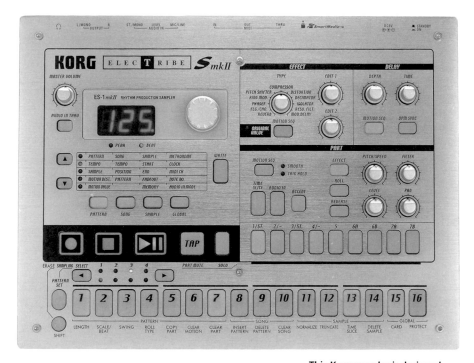

This Korg sampler is designed specifically for storing and sequencing music samples.

was unsuited for these problems, and even the record companies thought illegal sampling was nothing to worry about – or, at the very least, was uncontrollable.

In those days, for most DJs making records, producing a record went as follows:

- The DJ decided to use a sample from an old record for their new song.

- It sounded great and they started to wonder about their legal position.

- They ignored the problem, pressed up 500 'white label' 12-inch singles and sent them out to promoters and other DJs.

watch out!

Whenever you record a tune in a studio – at home or in an expensive posh studio – always leave the mixing process for another day. After a good sleep and a couple of days' recovery, your judgement will be better, more balanced and less inclined to personal indulgences.

- Sometimes they earned some money from selling a few – maybe enough to recoup what they had spent.

Now, from this point, the story usually went in one of three directions:

- The hype stopped – and no further copies were made. In this scenario, the DJ was pleased not to have paid out any money for lawyers' fees or any payment to the original artist as a 'sample clearance fee'. The sample and the record were forgotten about and they moved on to their next project; OR

- The hype carried on into a second round of pressing. The DJ sold all of the first lot and most of the second (and maybe even a third round) and it ended there – but the numbers were still small and no further copies were made. In this scenario, the total earnings were maybe as much as £3,000 and the DJ had made enough to do a new record and had built a bit of a local reputation. However, few people outside their fanbase knew about the record and, anyway, few people would have bothered suing for small amounts of money; OR

- The record exploded, the DJ was signed to a major record deal and swiftly became a Superstar DJ. At this point they may have begun to regret that they didn't act safely by clearing the sample in the first place. With their fast-rising profile, the likelihood of getting sued escalated massively. Suddenly they badly needed that lawyer they had earlier chosen not to call. However, since the vast majority of cases are settled before trial, their chances of ending up in court were always small. Even if they ended up paying a higher 'sample clearance fee' than they would have done, and incurred much higher legal fees, perhaps in the end they didn't really care in light of the happy position that their career had attained.

This may all sound a bit mercenary or even unethical – and it was, as was so much in those early days of dance music. However, things changed and the lawyers got clued up. Some musicians actually became lawyers themselves so that they could help their old friends with such problems. The laws were amended, people got sued and they lost so much time and money that, eventually, most of the business towed the line and began paying sample clearance fees.

The new scenarios are starkly split between those who pay the sample clearance fees and sleep at night and those who still act like cowboys. The latter generally live in fear that, if one of their sample-laden tunes becomes successful, the calls from the other side's lawyers will begin.

Of course, all this applies only to those unsigned artists who are recording privately with no recording agreement in place with anyone – as they are the only ones who actually have a choice. If you *do* have a deal of some kind, then you have no real choice other than to keep people fully informed and take no chances. As in life, those who take chances often get hit while the rest of us are more attractive for being able to get more sleep. Happy sampling.

want to know more?

- Go to: www.pointblanklondon.com for more information on music production for DJs.
- For 'GarageBand', see www.apple.com/support/downloads/garagebandjampack.html
- For 'ProTools', see www.digidesign.com/index.cfm?navid=24&langid=100&
- The three most popular and best programs (at least for DJs) are:
  o 'Logic' (http://www.apple.com/logicpro/)
  o 'Cubase' (http://www.steinbergusers.com/cubase/cubase.php)
  o 'Ableton Live' (http://www.ableton.com)

Glossary

A cappella
A song or mix containing only vocals, with no audible drums or other instruments.

Agent
A person who organizes a DJ's bookings, and usually takes about 10 per cent of the fee; also called a 'manager'.

Amplifier, Amp
A piece of equipment that increases the power of the signal from the mixer so that a pair (or pairs) of speakers are activated. Some speakers are 'self-powered,' with built-in amplifiers, but the majority will require a separate amp to operate.

Analogue
Old-style equipment. The opposite of digital.

Anti-skating
A feature found on professional turntables that prevents the needle from skipping across the record.

Aux (or Line in)
Abbreviation for 'auxiliary', meaning secondary or supplementary. In the case of DJ equipment such as a mixer or amplifier, the 'aux' input socket allows a secondary piece of equipment to be plugged in, e.g. a CD player. If you would like to record yourself mixing, your mixer should connect to the AUX socket on your hi-fi or stereo, and the 'record source' should be set to 'aux'.

Bar
A collection of beats in music. Usually there are four beats per bar in dance music.

Battle
A Hip Hop or Drum'n'Bass DJ competition in which DJs or MCs compete against each other in short sets showcasing their skills and taste.

Battle-style
A way of orienting the turntables in the DJ's set-up so that the tone arm sides of the decks are furthest away from the DJ, as opposed to the usual layout where the tone arm is to the right of the DJ. This method prevents the DJ's arms from brushing the tone arm and disrupting his mix in the heat of a battle.

Beat
A single pulse (or unit of rhythmical noise) in music. It can be made up of several notes or fractions of a note. The most common beats occur as four per bar (a '4/4' time signature).

Beat counter
An electronic device that counts the beats per minute (bpm) of a track.

Beat matching
The art of synchronizing two records, which have different speeds or tempos in time or in rhythm.

Beat juggling
This skill is done using two records and manipulating the arrangement of the elements (drum sounds, headnotes, vocals, etc.) from both to create a new-sounding track. For example, in a very simple beat juggle, one or more beats or bars of record 1 are played and the DJ then quickly flips the crossfader to the beat matched record 2 for one or more beats or bars, then back to 1 and so on.

Bias
When the crossfader or cue mix is at a higher volume or level on one channel it is said to be 'biased' to that channel. If the crossfader is more to the right-hand side, it is biased to the right channel.

Belt drive
One of the major differences in types of turntables is whether they are belt or direct drive. Belt drive turntables have their platter driven by a thick 'rubber band' compared to the more expensive type of turntable (direct drive)

which is driven by a motor (directly) without any intermediate component.

Blending

When a DJ mixes two tracks during the ambient or beatless part of one or both tracks, he is 'blending' the two tracks, as opposed to beat matching them or any other method of mixing of the two.

Body

The main section of a track, usually comprised of the theme including verses and choruses – between the intro and the breakdown.

BPM

'Beats Per Minute'. The bpm indicates the speed (or 'tempo') of an individual track. It is possible to determine the bpm of a track by counting the number of beats which occur in 60 seconds.

Break

The section of a track wherein the song generally fades down to an ambient, or beatless, section or the main rhythmic drums are reduced or left standing by the removal of the melody of the track, which can be seen on the vinyl as a smoother area.

Breakbeat, Breaks

This genre is characterized by a beat with a 'break' or gap in the continuity of the snare drums.

Breakdown

The section of a tune after the intro and before the outro where the beat thins out or stops, creating space and tension before the next section.

Build, build up

The section in a tune where the music develops melodic or rhythmic tension, before hitting the main Body or Breakdown of the tune.

Cartridge

The main part of the stylus or needle, attached to the end of the tone arm, where vibrations from the stylus are converted into electrical impulses.

Centre spindle

The blunt spike that points up in the middle of the platter.

Channel

One vertical section on a mixer, representing the input and output into the system of one source (e.g. turntable, CD player, etc.).

Channel fader

A slider or knob for each channel on the mixer that allows the DJ to control the individual volume of that channel.

Counterweight

The counterweight is situated towards the back of the tone arm and is responsible for the amount of pressure (or weight) the needle exerts on the record. If your needle is skipping it can help to increase the counterweight on it, but applying too much pressure can damage the record.

Crossfader, Fader, X-fader or Hamster switch

The key component of the DJ mixer, allowing the DJ to fade between individual channels or play two channels simultaneously.

Cueing

The act of finding the exact spot within the next record from which you intend to play, usually done in the headphones so that the audience cannot hear this preparatory activity.

Cue burn

Cueing a record repeatedly in one spot can wear down the groove in the record at that point, resulting in cue burn, which can cause the record to skip.

Cue level

The cue level controls the volume of sound playing through the headphones which the DJ hears to cue his next tune.

Cueing lever

A lever found on some decks to gently lower the needle onto the vinyl without scratching it – but never used by cooler DJs, who frown on such devices.

Cue mix
The cue mix allows you to hear what is being played on each channel through the headphones. You can also listen to both channels simultaneously and some mixers allow you to switch between the cue mix and what is currently being heard through the main speakers.

dB
A measurement of volume. Abbreviated as 'dB', this is the internationally-accepted unit for measurement of the volume level of sound.

Digital
Modern technology in format and equipment in which the data is stored as a string of numbers (1's and o's). The opposite of analogue.

Direct drive
One of the major types of turntables in which the platter is driven directly by the motor.

Downtempo
Slower, or relatively slow.

Drum'n'bass
The genre of speeded-up breakbeats and slower basslines.

EQ, Equalizer, Equalization
Two or three knobs on a mixer used to adjust the levels of bass, (maybe mid-range) and treble. There is often an EQ for each individual channel on the mixer.

Exit (or Outro)
As part of a track's structure, the exit is the last bars where several elements are usually dropped out to leave a simpler version of the track for easier mixing out.

Fader
A slider, usually the channel fader, but sometimes also the Master Output fader or the crossfader.

Filter
Another word for effects, with which a tune can be modified, e.g. flange, reverb, echo, etc.

Flight case
A record-carrying case designed to protect tunes from the effects of heat and rough handling during transit.

Gain
The amount by which an electronic circuit amplifies a signal. Sometimes used for 'volume'.

Genre
A single category (or 'style') of music, marked by a distinctive style, form and content.

Ground, grounding
The wire hanging from the back of a deck that needs to be connected to the grounding screw on the back of a mixer to prevent the 'hum' of feedback.

Hamster switch
A switch on some mixers that reverses the turntable so that the right channel swaps with the left to create effects. Sometimes simply the crossfader.

Headphones
Placed on your head so you can hear an incoming track while mixing, headphones are an essential part of DJing.

Headshell
The headshell joins directly onto the tone arm providing a protective housing unit for attachment of the cartridge.

Hi-fi
Short for high fidelity, formerly used to mean a home stereo set-up.

House
A genre of music with a four-bass-drums-per-bar beat of about 120 bpm. Sometimes the word refers simply to the main club or event space: 'The house volume is too low but these monitors are blowing my eardrums'.

Input selector
The input selector on the mixer is normally

found alongside the channel fader. The input selector enables you to switch from different input sources (e.g. another turntable or CD player).

Intro

The beginning section of a track, leading to the Body or a Breakdown.

Jungle

'The Jungle' was the name of a notorious area in the city of Kingston, Jamaica where Reggae and Dancehall beats evolved into what we now know as a form of Drum'n'Bass.

Junglist

A Jungle DJ or someone who enjoys Jungle or Drum'n'Bass.

Kill switch

The kill switch will instantly drop one channel's output, or the bass, mid-range or treble of a channel, out of the mix, and is useful for effects where the DJ drops one track out for a bar, or a beat or more. Kill switches accomplish this more cleanly than trying to slide the crossfader over quickly or the channel fader down fast.

Label

A record label – part of a (larger) record company that usually has many associated (or 'sister') labels. Also refers to the paper sticker on the middle of a record on which the artist name, title, and other information about the track are printed.

Levels

The relative amounts or volumes of highs, mids and bass sounds through the channels of a mixer. If asked by a sound engineer, the owner of the sound system or another interested party to 'check your levels', take it as a subtle hint that you are playing with too much volume or treble, bass, etc., and should adjust accordingly to improve the sound of your set.

Line or Aux

An input socket on mixers or high-quality audio equipment allowing line devices (such as CD players) to be connected.

Live

Playing 'live' is to produce music spontaneously with the use of synths, drum machines, etc., while DJing. (When used with reference to a turntable, if a deck is 'live' it is the one currently playing out through the house speakers.)

Loop

Part of a track's structure, a loop is usually made of 4–8 bars.

Master volume

The slider(s) or knob(s) on the mixer that controls the overall volume that will be pumped out via the amp through the speakers.

Minidisk

A small-format digital playback (and often recording) machine. Very useful as a recording machine at gigs (so you can check your performance later at home).

Mix

When two songs are mixed together using beat matching, beat juggling or a simple fade across the breaks in two tracks. Or simply the act of creating a mix. Or the final stage of producing a pop record in which the various sounds and elements are balanced and fine-tuned.

Mixer

One of the main tools, the mixer allows the DJ to combine two separate sound sources to play them as one.

Needle

Another term for a stylus.

Numark

Manufacturer of DJ equipment such as mixers and turntables.

Output display

The LED display that shows the level of the master volume (or sometimes of the channel volume).

Outro

Part of a track's structure, the outro is the last set of bars.

Panasonic

Panasonic is one of the world's leading manufacturers of audio equipment and makes the legendary Technics turntables, which are the industry standard.

Pick up time

The time taken for the platter to get up to the desired speed from a stopped position. This will largely depend on whether you are using belt or direct drive turntables.

Pitch

1. The relative position of a musical tone within the musical range ('high' or 'low').
2. The percentage speed at which a track is playing on a turntable, the pitch can be altered using the pitch control and is referred to as 'plus 4' or 'minus 6,' etc.

Pitch bend

On CD mixers the pitch bend (like a pitch control) allows the pitch of the track you are playing to be raised or lowered.

Pitch control

On turntables, the pitch control is a slider on the right-hand side allowing you to change the speed that the record is played. Typically the pitch can be altered up to +/- 8%

Platter

The circular metal plate that the motor drives or another term for a vinyl record.

Promo

A record that has not been officially released by a record label. It is commonly referred to as a 'white label' and is generally given to well-known DJs to play before the tune is released in order to generate hype.

Pushing off

When a DJ pushes the record off so that the beats will match with those on another deck as quickly as possible.

Quartz lock

A feature found on professional turntables to ensure the speed of the platter remains constant (or 'locked').

RPM

RPM stands for 'revolutions per minute' (the amount of times the record revolves in any given minute). There are two distinct types of records: 33rpm and 45rpm – though a third type (78rpm) is sometimes (if rarely) seen.

RPM adapter

Some vinyl, in particular those that are made to be played at 45 RPM, have a large hole cut out of the centre. (The reason for this extends back to the old days when vinyl was played in juke boxes.) In order for you to play these records on your turntables the adapter is placed on the centre spindle to increase the size.

Sample

A short sound; or an extracted sound or phrase from another source.

Sampler

A sort of synth or keyboard or computer program used to play pre-programmed samples by the pressing of buttons or keys.

Scratching

The sound produced when the vinyl is run back and forth under the needle, or a 'scratch' if a physical fault on a vinyl record or CD that adversely affects the sound.

Sennheiser

One of the leading manufacturers of audio equipment known especially for its lightweight headphones.

Seamless

This is used to describe the quality of a DJ's mixing. If done perfectly without faults or interruptions it is said to be seamless.

Selector

Also Selecta, Record Selector. A slang term for a DJ.

Skipping

When the tone arm is not correctly adjusted with enough pressure from the counter weight, the needle may slide (or 'skip') over the grooves in a record – the movement of people on the dancefloor (or a scratch) is often enough to create a skip.

Slipmat

A slipmat is the circular piece of felt placed between the platter and the record.

Spinback

Also known as a backspin, a spinback is performed by the DJ when he stops a record with his hand and rewinds it quickly.

Stylus

Commonly referred to as the needle, the stylus is in fact the tiny piece of metal (or diamond or other material) that reads the grooves of the record.

Target light

The target light is the small pop-up light on some decks that shines across the vinyl allowing the DJ to see in the dark how far into the record he has played, and where all the breakdowns are.

Techno

A genre of music featuring mechanical beats and recorded sounds that range from apocalyptic sirens to sampled TV and movie dialogue. It was developed in Detroit in the early Eighties and has a tempo of around 126–130 bpm.

Tempo

The speed of a track measured in bpm's (beats per minute).

Theme

In the structure of a track, themes are usually 4 to 32 bars and make up the main body of the tune, carry the melody and are the part fans usually hum when remembering a tune.

Tinnitus

The affliction of damage to the ears due to exposure to high volumes over extended periods.

Tone arm

The long metal arm attached at the top right-hand side of the turntable, to which the stylus and cartridge are also attached, which is usually S-shaped, although straight tone arms are supposed to prevent skipping.

Transform

A trick performed by the use of the crossfader or on/off switch to produce a very fast stuttering sound of the input source.

Vestax

One of the leading manufacturers of DJ equipment.

Vinyl

What records are made of, or another name for the records themselves.

Vocal

The singing or spoken voice part of a track.

Warping

If you leave your precious vinyls out in the sun or pack them too tightly in your crate, or stack them unevenly, they can warp, or bend – rendering them useless. You can attempt to fix your warped records by putting them on the turntable and using a hairdryer on a low setting to try and melt it back into shape.

Wax

Another name for records.

Wheels of steel

A name for turntables.

White label

A record that has no information on the label, which is generally a promo and given to well-known DJs to play before the tune is released in order to generate hype.

X-Fader

Another name used for the crossfader. It's the main component of the mixer, allowing you to fade between individual channels or play two channels simultaneously.

Need to know more?

If you would like to learn more about the world of DJing, your best bet is to go on a DJing course or befriend a couple of good DJs and learn 'on the job' with them, if they will let you. Alternatively, you can check out a whole host of other good books, useful websites and information on equipment manufacturers.

Further reading

Broughton, Frank and Brewster, Bill *How to DJ Right: The Art and Science of Playing Records* (Bantam Press, 2002). Two great DJs explain how DJs 'track down greatness and squeeze it together'.

Broughton, Frank and Brewster, Bill *Last Night a DJ Saved My Life: The History of the Disc Jockey* (Headline Ltd, 2006). The history of Dance Music and DJs crammed into one book.

Graudins, Charles, *How to Be a DJ* (Course Technology PTR, 2004). Loads of information about radio DJs, Mobile DJs and club DJs.

James, Ben and Webb, Gerald (Editor) *Digital DJ* (DJ Styles) (Alfred Publishing, 2003). Comprehensive guide to the world of Digital DJing.

Terret, Piper, *Bedroom DJ*, (Omnibus Press, 2003) Helpful and easy-to-read guide to the proper basics.

Zemon, Stacy, *The Mobile DJ Handbook: How to Start & Run a Profitable Mobile Disc Jockey Service* (Focal Press, 2002). Said to be the biggest-selling book ever on DJing and written for 'the aspiring DJ beginning his or her new business'.

Zemon, Stacy *The DJ Sales and Marketing Handbook: How to Achieve Success, Grow Your Business, and Get Paid to Party!* (Focal Press, 2005). A useful sourcebook for all DJs, which aims to be 'a roadmap to maximizing your profits' as a DJ.

A selection of useful websites

www.pointblanklondon.com
www.apple.com/support/downloads/
  garagebandjampack.html
www.digidesign.com
www.apple.com/logicpro/
www.steinbergusers.com/cubase/
  cubase.php
www.stantondj.com
www.panasonic.co.uk/technics-dj-
  home/index.htm
www.technics1210.com
www.dj-tips-and-tricks.com/
www.djdownload.com
www.beatport.com
www.mixmag.net
www.crossfader.com
www.beatmixing.com
www.clubdjzone.com
www.harmony-central.com/Effects/
  Articles/Equalization
www.music.columbia.edu/cmc/
  courses/g6630/Equalization.html

www.bangingtunes.com
www.discjockey101.com
www.djkeltech.com/scratch.htm
www.i-dj.co.uk/technique/
  techniquepage.php?ID=10
www.mp3machine.com/win/MIXING_DJ
www.mymusictools.com/download/dj
www.pcdj.com
www.ableton.com

Equipment manufacturers and suppliers

Ableton
Apple
Beatport
Beyer
Digidesign
Final Scratch
Microsoft
Sennheiser
Stanton
Technics – Panasonic
Vestax

Index

Acknowledgements

The author and publishers would like to thank the following individuals and organizations for the use of their photographs in this book: Apple Macintosh (page 18); DJ Tu-Ki (page 157); Korg (page 179); Ministry of Sound (pages 33, 34, 87, 91, 99, 106, 113, 158, 159); Diarmuid Moloney/Focus Publishing (pages 11, 43, 49, 51, 53, 58, 63, 76, 77, 84, 86, 93, 96, 97, 98, 102, 109, 111, 128, 129, 150, 154, 173); Numark (pages 37, 41, 42, 73); Pioneer (pages 40, 41, 45); Point Blank (pages 12, 135, 137, 170, 175); Solo (page 19); Loughlin Sweeney/Choice Cuts (pages 8, 13, 83, 88, 105, 124, 130, 142, 157, 164); Technics (pages 15, 108); Vestax (page 22). All other images were supplied by the author.

About the author

UK-based American-born Tom Frederikse has been a record producer since the birth of DJ Culture in 1988. He has worked on over 100 UK Top 40 records for such varied artists as Robbie Williams, Michael Jackson and James Brown, and has worked with many of the best British and American DJs, including Sasha, Allister Whitehead, Joey Negro, Tommy D, Frankie Foncett, Marshall Jefferson and Bam Bam.

◌ Collins need to know?

Look out for these recent titles in Collins' practical and accessible need to know? series.

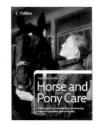

Other titles in the series:

To order any of these titles, please telephone 0870 787 1732 quoting reference 263H. For further information about all Collins books, visit our website: www.collins.co.uk